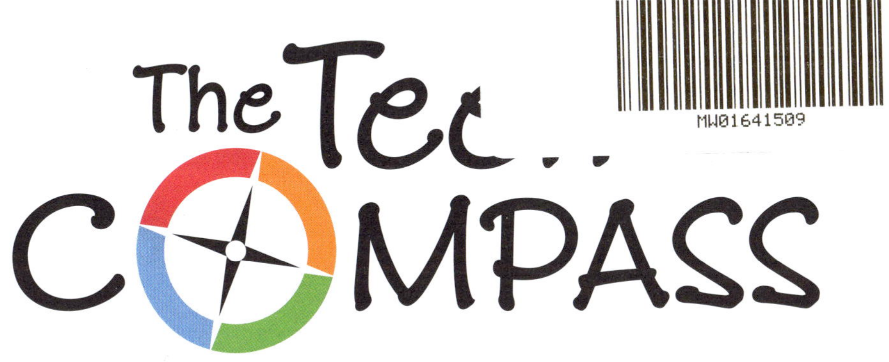

Faith and Wellness Notebook

Updated Edition

The Rev. Dr. D. Scott Stoner, LMFT
& Holly Hughes Stoner, LMFT

We wish to express our deep gratitude to our friends
Ab and Nancy Nicholas
for their faithful and generous support.

We have created a ***Leader's Guide*** to accompany this Notebook.

To find out more and to order: livingcompass.org

Find us on the web: livingcompass.org

Connect with us on Facebook and Twitter

Questions? Email us: holly@livingcompass.org

ISBN Print edition: 978-1-944146-08-5
ISBN Digital edition: 978-1-944146-09-2
1. Teens 2. Faith and Wellness 3. Christian life 4. Spiritual
I. Title
Printed in the United States of America.

The Teen Compass Faith and Wellness Notebook

I have used The Teen Compass Faith and Wellness Notebook *with our group and the feedback has been very positive. The discussions that arise from the notebook have been very beneficial to the youth. It helps create a safe and fun space for them as they identify their own strengths and weaknesses, and set goals that enable them to live into their best hopes for themselves.*

—***The Rev. Joshua Hill,*** Ethics teacher, *Episcopal School of Knoxville,* Knoxville, Tennessee

The Teen Compass Faith and Wellness Notebook *has been one of the best tools I've found for preparing teens for confirmation because it allows them to openly explore their beliefs as Christians, and provides a space to contemplate how those beliefs apply to every aspect of their lives. It allows them to ask deep questions about faith and their lives and share those thoughts with others. Perhaps most valuable to me is that they learn the important skill of self-reflection through the Self-Assessments. Teens have told me how they go back to the assessments, especially when they feel "stuck," because they help them find direction.*

—***The Rev. Deborah Woolsey,*** *Episcopal Church of the Good Shepherd,* Athens, Ohio

Through The Teen Compass Faith and Wellness *program, which we used at a youth retreat, teens are discovering how to reach deeper within themselves. They are beginning to recognize when something is "off" or out of balance in their lives, and then how to navigate to wellness. And perhaps for the first time, with the tools provided by The Teen Compass, teens are realizing that they possess within themselves that which they need to be wholly healthy. After the retreat, the teens expressed that* The Teen Compass Faith and Wellness *program had made an impact on them, and that they felt more empowered to seek wellness within their entire being.*

—***Crystal Tidmore,*** Director of Fellowship and Formation, *Good Shepherd on the Hill: a second campus of the Episcopal Church of the Good Shepherd,* Austin, Texas

Using The Teen Compass Faith and Wellness *program in our community groups has allowed every member of faculty and staff to engage our students in conversations of character development. Not only did our students begin seeing connections between the four pillars at the school, but faculty and staff now shared a common language to speak about raising whole young men and began to better understand how our life in community is integral to the raising of our boys.*

—***Jennifer Henery,*** Director of Spiritual Life and Character Development, *St. John's Northwestern Military Academy,* Delafield, Wisconsin

Our teens have found an important and unique resource in The Teen Compass Faith and Wellness *program. With all of the demands placed on teens in high functioning families and schools, the invitation to stop and take care of their whole selves has challenged them to think about what they are, and are not, doing with their time. It is a skill-set and way of thinking our teens have never before considered. We can see them taking deep internal notes that they will rely on as they grow into themselves.* The Teen Compass Faith and Wellness *program—like a set of forms for a poured concrete basement—helps teens create the shape and outline of the foundation on which beautiful lives can be built.*

—**The Rev. Canon Jadon D. Hartsuff,** *Saint John's Cathedral,* Denver, Colorado

Contents

Introducing *The Teen Compass Faith and Wellness Notebook*

An emerging adult or teen, like yourself, is making one of the most amazing transformations in all of life. You are in the midst of changing from a child—having learned from everything that the adults in your world exposed you to—into an adult. Figuratively speaking, up until now, you have been going through life riding in the passenger seat of the car. Adults have been driving the car and everywhere the adults went, you went as well. Things are beginning to change now. You are the one who is beginning to drive your life. You are moving into the driver's seat and are beginning to make very important decisions about where the car, your life, will be going, what kind of a driver you will be, and who will be in the car with you. You are transforming into an adult and are making small decisions each day that add up, determining much of what your adult life will look like.

Most young people yearn for the day when they will be adults, with no one looking over their shoulders, telling them what to do and what not to do. Most young people have been looking forward for a long time to having the freedom to make more decisions for themselves. Adulthood truly is awesome and does allow for much more freedom. However, this freedom comes with many important new responsibilities and endless new decisions that will soon be your own. The decisions that you as a teen, make each day, create the building blocks of your adult life.

This *Teen Compass Faith and Wellness Notebook* was created to help you take a look at your life and help you think about how you feel about the direction your life is going. Just as people use a compass to help check their bearings and make sure they are headed in the direction they intend, this notebook will do the same for you in regards to the choices you are making in your life. More importantly, this notebook will help you to become more intentional about the choices you make going forward and will help you make sure you are headed in the direction you really want for yourself.

Eight important areas of wellness in your life are covered in this notebook:

Spirituality

Stress Resilience

Relationships

Rest and Play

Handling Emotions

Organization

School and Work

Care for the Body

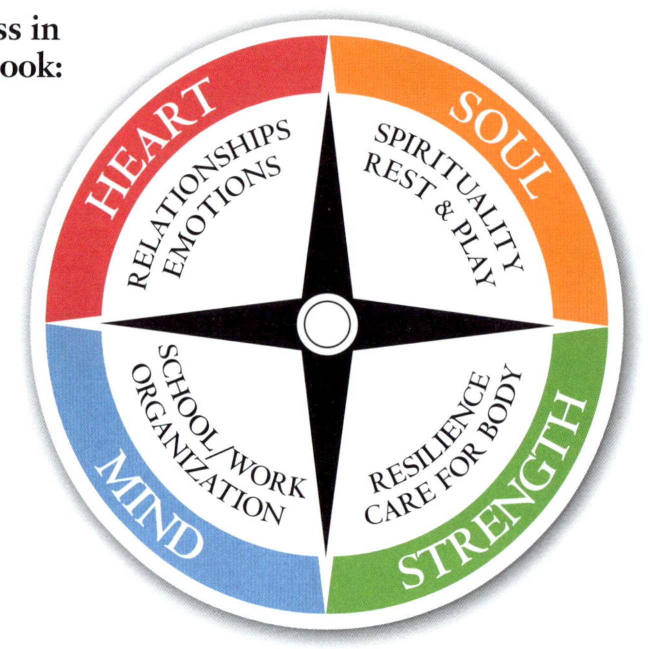

You will be invited in each unit to complete a Self-Assessment related to these areas of wellness. Are you living a life full of energy, focus and possibility, or are you sitting back and letting life unfold before you, as chance would have it? You will also be invited to slow down and reflect on whether the life you are living now is the life God desires for you. Does God, the quiet whisper that surrounds you, give you an uncomfortable feeling or does God celebrate with you that you are creating a life of meaning and purpose?

The National Wellness Institute defines wellness as "an active process through which people become aware of, and make choices toward, a more successful existence." Personal wellness occurs when one commits to a continuous, lifelong process of developing a lifestyle based on healthy attitudes and actions. The wellness process consists of increasing awareness and choosing options that result in growth and balance among the eight primary areas. As God's people, we want to live our lives in a way that is congruent with God's teachings. This notebook is a tool created just for you. As you begin the journey into adulthood, it will provide a compass—a living compass—to help you navigate your way.

Enjoy this important time of your life. Have fun exploring your new freedoms and taking care of yourself and your life.

The Teen Compass Self-Assessment Tool

Once you have arrived at your total score from each Self-Assessment, shade in that section of the compass (0 is at the center, 50 is halfway out, and 100 is at the outer edge). Use a pencil, pen, or crayons to shade in each area with your total score (see pages 4 and 5 for examples). Your scores are not "good" or "bad," nor are they "strong" or "weak." They are simply a current snapshot of what areas of your life you have been paying the most attention to, and those areas that might be in need of a little more of your attention and commitment in order for you to be healthier.

The Teen Compass Self-Assessment

Sample Scores

Organization

The ability to keep track of and make good use of time, priorities, money, and possessions.

Rate the following 10 statements from 0–10 based on the scale below, and then write your responses on the lines provided. When you are finished, add up your responses and then shade in the total score in the **Organization** section of the Compass Self-Assessment Tool on page 3. (See pages 4 and 5 for examples.)

e		Most of the Time		Always
6	7	8	9	10

track of my money.	7
nmitments.	6
t I allow enough	6
nsuring that I have of my life.	7
ignments and other	4
l, and I can get my	5
sessions so that I do	6
s in a healthy way.	6
y own laundry, help track of important papers.	6
do that day.	7
TOTAL	60

you see one area that could use more ould benefit or improve your life? Think u feel willing to commit to over the next nething that you really feel is important he next page, and then share aloud with Oriented, Inspired, Time Sensitive, and s and a sample FAITH Step.)

Handling Emotions

The ability to express your emotions and to receive others' emotions in a healthy way.

Rate the following 10 statements from 0–10 based on the scale below, and then write your responses on the lines provided. When you are finished, add up your responses and then shade in the total score in the **Handling Emotions** section of the Compass Self-Assessment Tool on page 3. (See pages 4 and 5 for examples.)

Never		Sometimes		Half of the Time			Most of the Time			Always
0	1	2	3	4	5	6	7	8	9	10

Statement	Score
People who know me would say I handle my emotions in a healthy way.	10
I avoid using alcohol, other drugs, and other possibly addictive behaviors to deal with my emotions.	8
The way I show my emotions demonstrates respect toward myself and others.	10
I feel good about the way I handle my emotions and how that affects my relationships.	8
I have a solid and healthy sense of confidence in myself.	7
I know the early warning signs of depression or anxiety and would feel comfortable seeking help from a trusted person if I felt this way.	10
I am able to share my full range of emotions (including sadness, happiness, fear, and worry) with people I trust.	10
I am able to communicate my emotions in a positive way without being irritable, critical, or angry.	8
When someone I care about is upset, I am comfortable listening and really being present to them.	9
When I am feeling emotionally overwhelmed, I can turn to God and prayer to re-center myself.	10
TOTAL	90

Looking carefully at the scores you gave yourself, do you see one area that could use more attention, one area that if you paid more attention to it would benefit or improve your life? Think concretely as you create a FAITH Step for yourself that you feel willing to commit to over the next several weeks. This is only for you, so make sure it is something that you really feel is important to you and fits who you are. Write your FAITH Step on the next page, and then share aloud with at least one person. List one step that is: Focused, Action Oriented, Inspired, Time Sensitive, and Heartfelt and Honest. (See pages 6 and 7 for instructions and a sample FAITH Step.)

The Teen Compass Self-Assessment Tool

Sample Results Based on Total Scores

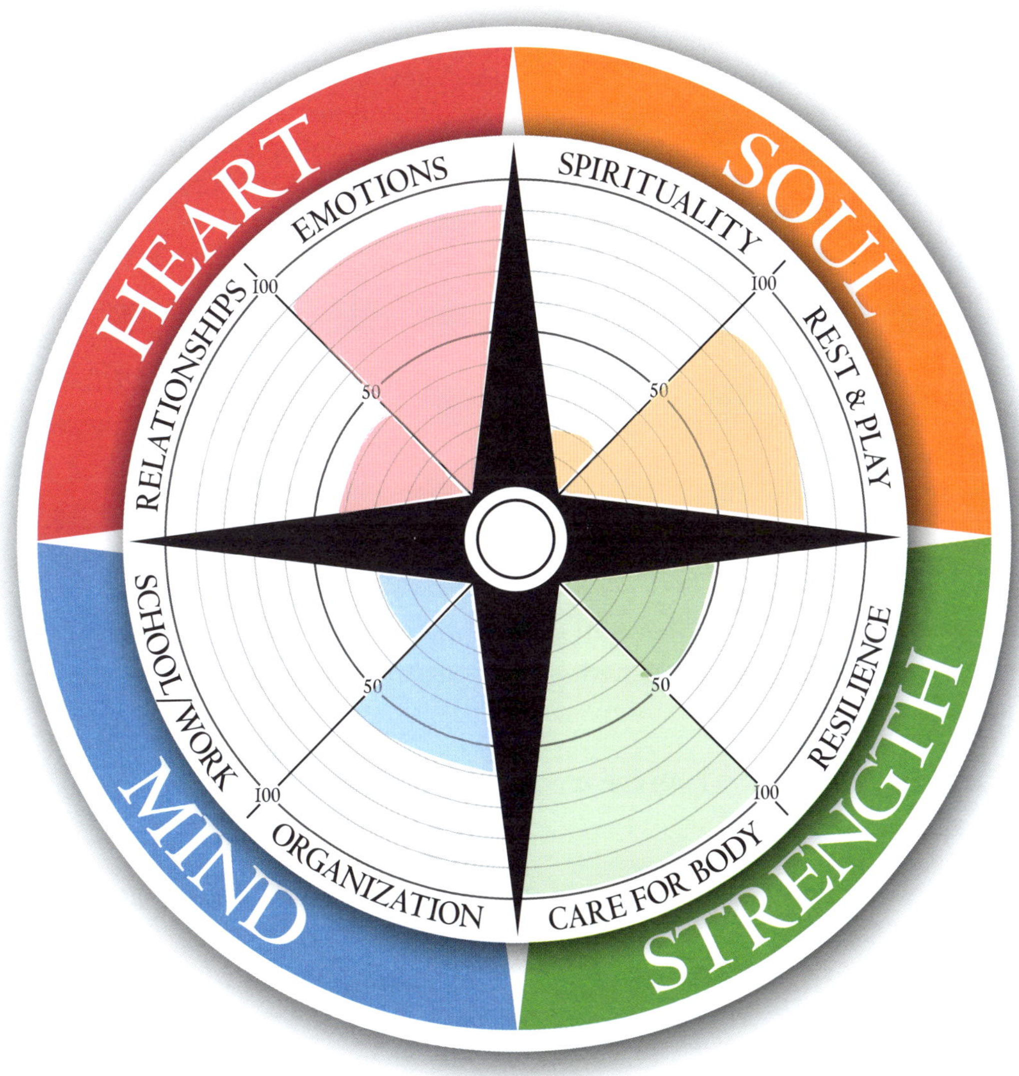

FAITH Steps

Your journey toward living a healthy, satisfying, and meaningful life happens one step at a time. Research shows that in order to maximize your chances for making positive changes, you need to break down those changes into small, concrete steps. And then share the change you want to make aloud with at least one other person.

A FAITH Step will help you identify those small steps you are ready to take, and offer the support you'll need to make a positive change. Here's how. Once you've shaded in your scores from the Self-Assessments on your own compass, you will be invited to identify one thing you can commit to doing that could improve your score (see sample on facing page). To help you, we've included a section in each Unit for you to write down a FAITH Step for each of the eight areas of wellness.

CHARACTERISTICS OF FAITH STEPS AND HOW TO CREATE YOUR OWN

F **Focused**
For example: I will **walk for 30 minutes three days this week** *vs.* I need to start getting some exercise.

A **Action Oriented**
For example: **I will walk three days this week.**

I **Inspired**
For example: I have wanted to do this **for a long time** as I know it will help reduce my stress *vs.* I know I should get more exercise because everyone says I should.

T **Time Sensitive**
For example: I will do it **between now and a week from now**.

H **Heartfelt and Honest**
For example: Exercise is something **I** really care about and **I** feel strongly will make a difference in my life.

Example of a FAITH Step

Area of Wellness: Care for the Body

Date: 8/23

Overarching Goal: I need to get more exercise.

Focused: I will walk for 30 minutes three days this week.

Action: I will walk three days this week.

Inspired: I have wanted to do this for a long time because I know it will help reduce my stress.

Time Sensitive: I will start between now and a week from now.

Heartfelt and Honest: I really care about how I feel and I strongly believe that exercise will make a difference in my life.

Obstacles: I do not have time in my current routine to do this.

Solutions: I will spend less time on Facebook or playing video games and go for a walk instead.

Final FAITH Step: Because I want to feel good and have less stress, for the next 2 weeks, beginning tomorrow, I will walk 30 minutes 3 days a week.

Use the space below to reflect on this section. Remember: what you write is private, and nobody should see it unless you want to share it with them.

UNIT 1

Spirituality

Don't become so well adjusted to your culture that you fit into it without even thinking. Instead, fix your attention on God. You'll be changed from the inside out.

— Romans 12:2 (The Message)

SECTION ONE: **Listening to Yourself**

Imagine a great, tall tree growing somewhere. Trees that are very large are often very old. To reach old age, trees need to be able to weather a multitude of seasons and a multitude of changes—changes in their environment, such as severe storms, droughts, and floods. To be able to survive those outside forces, a tree needs to have a good, well-developed root system—roots that not only run deep, but also reach out far beyond the trunk of the tree. A well-developed root system helps a tree to bend in a raging wind and a well-developed root system can find water in a drought. A well-developed root system keeps a tree healthy and growing as it keeps the tree grounded and connected to the earth.

What is true for trees is also true for people. We need a strong root system to sustain us through the many changes in life. For us, our root system is our faith or spiritual life. You undoubtedly will face challenges, disappointments and difficult periods in your life ahead. You will also have moments of joy, wonder, and pleasure. Life is complex and mysterious. Your faith will help you keep perspective and give you strength through all of it.

Take a few minutes now and complete the following Spirituality Self-Assessment. This is your assessment, no one else needs to see it or read it unless you want them to. It is for you and you alone, a chance for you to step back and take a look at the spiritual part of your life. How strong is your root system right now?

Be honest with yourself, and be gentle with yourself. There are no right or wrong answers; the results do not make you a good or a bad person. You are who you are; this is just one way for you to see where you are right now in the spiritual part of your life. Don't spend too much time thinking about each answer, just enough to give an honest answer so that you can use this later on.

Spirituality

The ability to live out our faith in everyday life.

Rate the following 10 statements from 0–10 based on the scale below, and then write your responses on the lines provided. When you are finished, add up your responses and then shade in the total score in the **Spirituality** section of the Compass Self-Assessment Tool on page 3. (See pages 4 and 5 for examples.)

Never		Sometimes		Half of the Time			Most of the Time			Always
0	1	2	3	4	5	6	7	8	9	10

I may not know what I want to do yet with my life, but I know my life has meaning and purpose. _____

I feel that the ways I give back to the world please God. _____

I have a strong sense of God's presence in my life. _____

I forgive myself and others as my faith teaches me to do. _____

I seek forgiveness from family and friends when I have hurt them. _____

I have activities that I do regularly to renew my soul, to center myself, and to gain perspective. _____

I am a part of a community that enriches my spiritual life. _____

The way I am living my life is consistent with my Christian values. _____

I thank God for the good things in my life. _____

My spiritual life informs the way I live my life. _____

TOTAL _____

Looking carefully at the scores you gave yourself, do you see one area that could use more attention, one area that if you paid more attention to it would benefit or improve your life? Think concretely as you create a FAITH Step for yourself that you feel willing to commit to over the next several weeks. This is only for you, so make sure it is something that you really feel is important to you and fits who you are. Write your FAITH Step on the next page, and then share aloud with at least one person. List one step that is: Focused, Action Oriented, Inspired, Time Sensitive, and Heartfelt and Honest. (See pages 6 and 7 for instructions and a sample FAITH Step.)

Create a FAITH Step

Area of Wellness: Spirituality

Date: ____________

Overarching Goal:
Focused: **A**ction: **I**nspired: **T**ime Sensitive: **H**eartfelt and Honest:

Obstacles:	Solutions:

Final FAITH Step:

SECTION TWO: **Learning**

Just like that tree that was mentioned earlier, we need to be grounded in order to grow and thrive through all the changes of life. If you aren't going through changes right now, rest-assured, they are ahead. Life guarantees it. Some changes can be fun and exciting; others can be challenging. Some are unexpected and unwanted; others are planned and welcomed. But even good changes can take some getting used to. It's the nature of change.

To be as grounded as that tree, you need to develop your own root system: one that goes deep and reaches out beyond yourself. **Spirituality is the part of this notebook where you work at deepening and enriching your life through experiences that help you strengthen your awareness of, and relationship with, God.** By deepening your relationship with God you will become more deeply grounded in something other than yourself, and will be better prepared for any tough times that might come your way. Like all things, spirituality must be practiced for it to grow.

Here are some suggestions for spiritual practices you might want to try to help deepen and enrich your spiritual life:

- Pick a prayer that is meaningful to you, and pray it regularly.
- Write your own prayer to pray at a certain time of day each day.
- Listen to or sing songs that help you feel close to God. Be creative. Write music, paint or draw something, write a story or other creative piece, take photos, do something that unleashes your creative side. Be grateful for your ability to do so.
- Go for a walk or run. When you find the right place sit, pray, or take in God's creation before returning home.
- Give back to the community.

Another spiritual practice that is easy to do is journaling. Journaling is more than just a chance to write down what you liked or didn't like about a day. When you journal you have the opportunity to engage in holy conversation with yourself and God. Like most things, journaling takes time and practice to make it feel natural. A great place to start journaling is to write about things that you are grateful for from your day. Paying attention to the simple things that you might otherwise take for granted is a great spiritual practice.

You may also want to try meditation. For many people this sounds intimidating, but you certainly can do it. It takes intention and practice and has been used by people of all ages from all over the world to help them listen to God, and to their own hearts. Like many things, it isn't as difficult as it seems once you get started. **Meditation only means setting aside a few minutes on a regular basis: once a day, twice a week, whenever, to be still and quiet, listening to God and to your heart.** Being quiet means not only being silent, but refusing to listen to the "voices" of social media, the news, Facebook, texts, commercials, or songs you listen to in order to refocus yourself—mind, body, heart, and soul—on God. It can be really hard to turn off all that "noise," but when practiced, meditation can help you step out of the swirl of the world and listen to God.

You might want to try what is known as a "breath prayer." A breath prayer is a way to do meditation while focusing on your breath. As you sit somewhere quiet, breathe in, saying to yourself, "Peace before me," then breathe out as you say, "Peace behind me," then breathe in again and say, "Peace above me." Keep going. You don't need to breathe differently than you normally do when you practice this. Just relax and breathe.

You can also use walking as a way of doing centering prayer, which is great for people who like to be active while praying. Take a walk, but leave your phone and other distractions behind. With each step, think of yourself as a child of God. Remember that God is with you. If you are upset, this can be a helpful way to not only calm down, but also to begin to let go of what is making you upset.

Jesus modeled the importance of taking time to deepen our relationship with God. Scripture tells us that he frequently retreated from the crowds to pray, to renew himself for what was ahead for him to face.

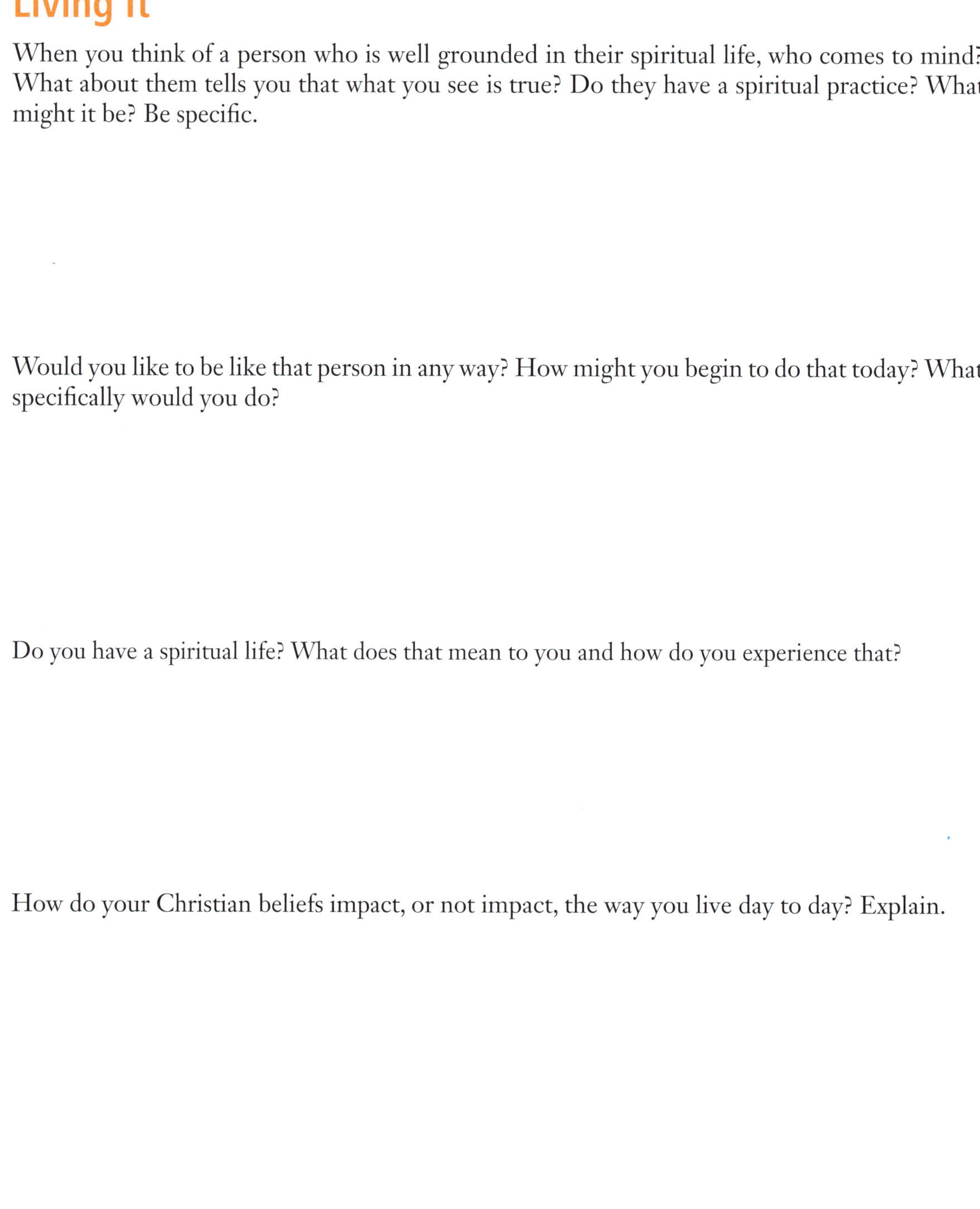

Living It

When you think of a person who is well grounded in their spiritual life, who comes to mind? What about them tells you that what you see is true? Do they have a spiritual practice? What might it be? Be specific.

Would you like to be like that person in any way? How might you begin to do that today? What specifically would you do?

Do you have a spiritual life? What does that mean to you and how do you experience that?

How do your Christian beliefs impact, or not impact, the way you live day to day? Explain.

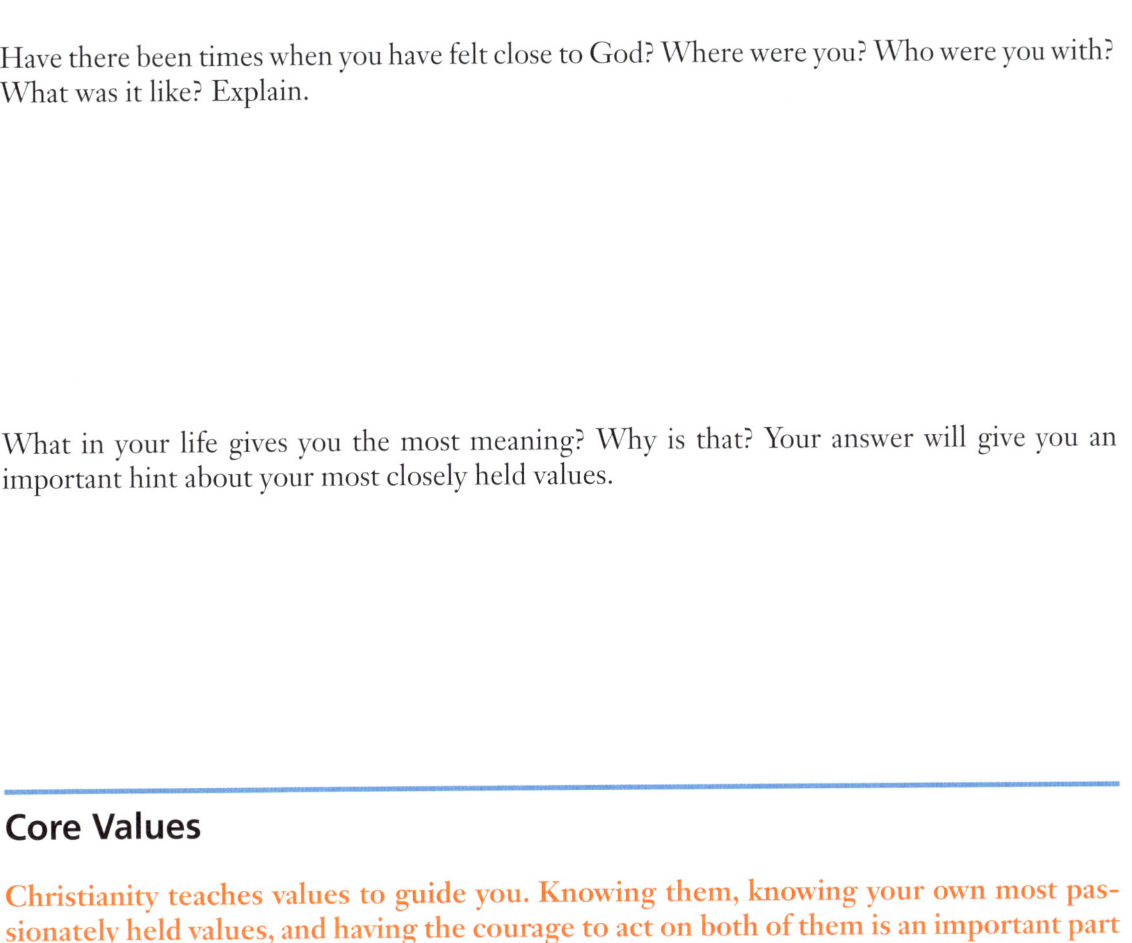

Have there been times when you have felt close to God? Where were you? Who were you with? What was it like? Explain.

What in your life gives you the most meaning? Why is that? Your answer will give you an important hint about your most closely held values.

Core Values

Christianity teaches values to guide you. Knowing them, knowing your own most passionately held values, and having the courage to act on both of them is an important part of your spirituality, as your values guide how you live your life.

The following exercise will help you clarify your core values. It is a challenging exercise, and it will be more meaningful if you do it silently, slowly, and on your own.

Identify the values that are most important to you. Do that gradually by striking through values from the list that are less important to you. This does not mean that you are throwing values away or don't care about them. The ones you cross out may still be important but won't be the most important to you. The narrowing process helps you determine your CORE values. The goal is to eventually narrow your list to **three values** that you hold as most important now. If a value that you hold is not on the list, please feel free to add it.

Pay attention to your inner dialogue as you narrow the list to three. Your process will reveal interesting truths about yourself.

List of Values

acceptance	attractiveness	community	contribution	ecology
family	fun	helpfulness	humor	intimacy
logic	pleasure	responsibility	self-esteem	stability
tradition	wisdom	accuracy	authority	comfort
courtesy	excellence	flexibility	generosity	honesty
independence	justice	gentleness	popularity	risk
self- knowledge	strength	virtue	success	achievement
beauty	patience	compassion	creativity	faithfulness
forgiveness	growth	hope	hard work	knowledge
moderation	power	safety	service	faith/spirituality
wealth	adventure	authenticity	caring	honor
love	dependability	fame	friendship	health
humility	peace	leisure	loyalty	orderliness
practicality	self-control	simplicity	tolerance	work ethic
gratitude	kindness	truth	integrity	____________

After you have narrowed down your values, think about whether those around you can tell that those values are important to you. Write here about how you show the world, by the way you live, that those values are so important to you. Give examples.

List your three most important core values.

1. ______________________________

2. ______________________________

3. ______________________________

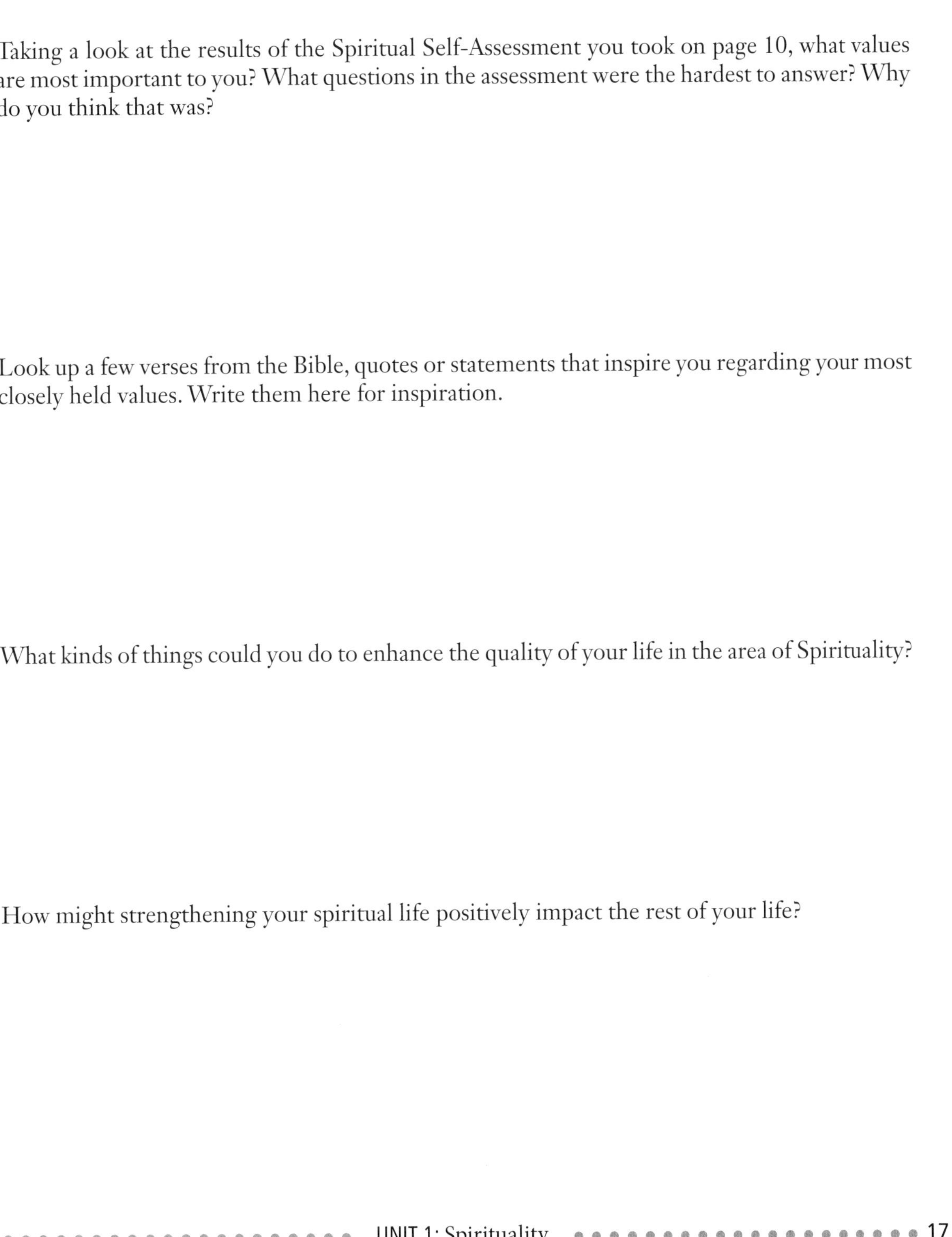

Taking a look at the results of the Spiritual Self-Assessment you took on page 10, what values are most important to you? What questions in the assessment were the hardest to answer? Why do you think that was?

Look up a few verses from the Bible, quotes or statements that inspire you regarding your most closely held values. Write them here for inspiration.

What kinds of things could you do to enhance the quality of your life in the area of Spirituality?

How might strengthening your spiritual life positively impact the rest of your life?

SECTION THREE: **Making the Connection**

But he answered, "It is written, 'One does not live by bread alone, but by every word that comes from the mouth of God.'"

— Matthew 4:4

If any think they are religious, and do not bridle their tongues but deceive their hearts, their religion is worthless. Religion that is pure and undefiled before God, the Father, is this: to care for orphans and widows in their distress, and to keep oneself unstained by the world.

— James 1:26-27

You must understand this, my beloved: let everyone be quick to listen, slow to speak, slow to anger; for your anger does not produce God's righteousness. Therefore rid yourselves of all sordidness and rank growth of wickedness, and welcome with meekness the implanted word that has the power to save your souls.

— James 1:19-21

Take a look at the scripture verses here, and in the last section. How can they help guide and inspire you as you live your life?

Do any of these verses have your name on it? How does it apply to you personally?

Are there other verses that might help guide you? Give examples.

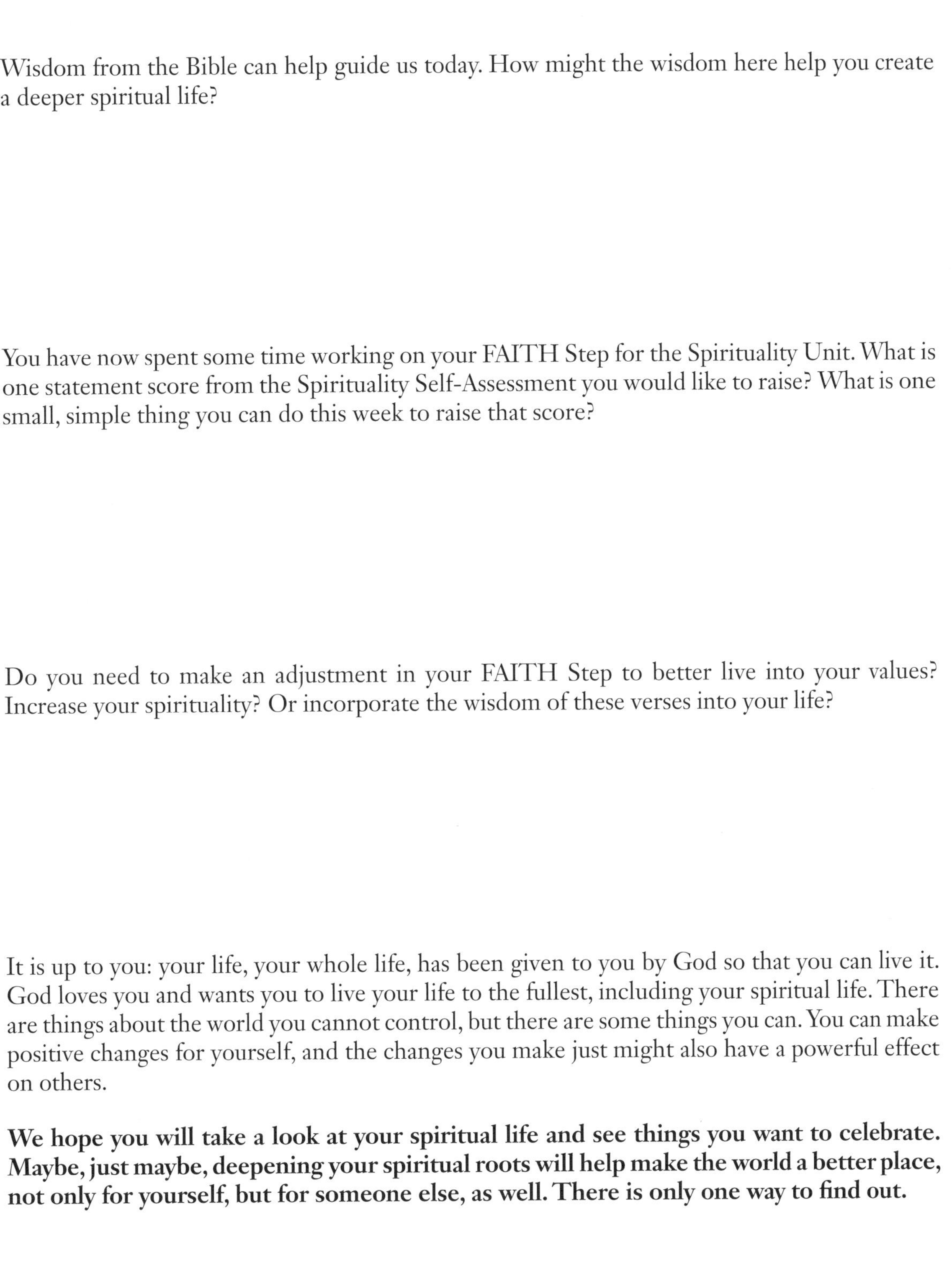

Wisdom from the Bible can help guide us today. How might the wisdom here help you create a deeper spiritual life?

You have now spent some time working on your FAITH Step for the Spirituality Unit. What is one statement score from the Spirituality Self-Assessment you would like to raise? What is one small, simple thing you can do this week to raise that score?

Do you need to make an adjustment in your FAITH Step to better live into your values? Increase your spirituality? Or incorporate the wisdom of these verses into your life?

It is up to you: your life, your whole life, has been given to you by God so that you can live it. God loves you and wants you to live your life to the fullest, including your spiritual life. There are things about the world you cannot control, but there are some things you can. You can make positive changes for yourself, and the changes you make just might also have a powerful effect on others.

We hope you will take a look at your spiritual life and see things you want to celebrate. Maybe, just maybe, deepening your spiritual roots will help make the world a better place, not only for yourself, but for someone else, as well. There is only one way to find out.

Use the space below to reflect on this section. Remember: what you write is private, and nobody should see it unless you want to share it with them.

UNIT 2

Stress Resilience

God of Peaceful Hearts, You know when my life becomes hectic and overwhelming, when nothing goes the way I want. You know when I am struggling with a history assignment, a math test, or a chemistry quiz. Often I lose my way, my sense of priorities. A quick prayer can bring me back to you. When I pray, things tend to calm down, and I realize I can handle anything if I just keep in touch with you. Let me make an effort to "roll with life's punches." Today I will keep in touch with you all day long through short prayers. I will not let the pressures get the upper hand.

—Danielle, age 17

SECTION ONE: **Listening to Yourself**

Your life is full. There is a lot to do in school, at home, with your friends, and at work. Everyone has expectations of you. Some are to do the best you can do and to be the best you can be every day. Some expectations are that you will think and act a certain way. Sometimes those expectations can build up. Sometimes things don't work out the way you want them to. You can get frustrated. You can feel pressure. That is stress. It is everywhere.

Everyone has stress. There is no place we can go to get away from it. But we don't have to let it overwhelm us. We don't have to let stress "stress us out." Stress is part of life for everyone. Like all aspects of life, we will be better off if we learn skills to help us work through stressful times so they don't take over our heart, soul, strength, and mind. Our faith can help us, too, as it helps us keep things in perspective and reminds us of what is truly important.

Take a few minutes and complete the following Stress Resilience Self-Assessment. Answer each question honestly; this is just for you, a chance for you to listen to yourself, to see where you are in term of handling the stress in your life.

Stress Resilience

The ability to deal positively with the adversities of life.

Rate the following 10 statements from 0–10 based on the scale below, and then write your responses on the lines provided. When you are finished, add up your responses and then shade in the total score in the **Stress Resilience** section of the Compass Self-Assessment Tool on page 3. (See pages 4 and 5 for examples.)

Never		Sometimes		Half of the Time			Most of the Time			Always
0	1	2	3	4	5	6	7	8	9	10

I feel good that things going on in my personal life rarely interfere with my concentration at school or work. _____

I respond to changes in my life with a positive attitude. _____

When I am stressed or in the midst of a challenge in my life, I turn to God and my faith to give me strength and perspective. _____

I feel good about the support I get from others when I have something big going on in my life. _____

When I face a life challenge, I turn to God and others to help me handle the accompanying stress in a healthy way. _____

When I have problems, I am able to keep them in perspective. _____

When I have a problem, I turn to others for support rather than keeping it to myself. _____

I am satisfied with the way I handle stress, handling it in healthy ways rather than coping by engaging in self-destructive habits. _____

In the past month, I have been free from any symptoms such as trouble sleeping, headaches, outbursts of anger, or feelings of depression that may be related to stress. _____

I am dealing well with any major life changes, planned or unplanned, that have occurred over the last few years in my life. _____

TOTAL _____

Looking carefully at the scores you gave yourself, do you see one area that could use more attention, one area that if you paid more attention to it would benefit or improve your life? Think concretely as you create a FAITH Step for yourself that you feel willing to commit to over the next several weeks. This is only for you, so make sure it is something that you really feel is important to you and fits who you are. Write your FAITH Step on the next page, and then share aloud with at least one person. List one step that is: Focused, Action Oriented, Inspired, Time Sensitive, and Heartfelt and Honest. (See pages 6 and 7 for instructions and a sample FAITH Step.)

Create a FAITH Step

Area of Wellness: Stress Resilience

Date: ______

Overarching Goal:

Focused:

Action:

Inspired:

Time Sensitive:

Heartfelt and Honest:

Obstacles:	Solutions:

Final FAITH Step:

SECTION TWO: Learning

Strangely enough, we can learn something important about stress from frogs. You may have heard that if you put a frog in a pot of cold water and put that pot over a flame, gradually heating the water, the frog will not jump out. Eventually, the frog will allow itself to be boiled to death, seemingly unaware of the heat slowly rising around it. Some students did this experiment and tried dropping frogs into water that was already hot. Each one of those frogs jumped out immediately! Apparently people are much like frogs. When things heat up around us gradually, we don't pay it much attention, yet if something stressful comes out of nowhere, we are more likely to deal with it right away.

It is true that warning signs about stress building up in our lives usually come slowly, gradually. The first sign that stress is hurting us usually comes in a "whisper," a quiet murmur, or a hint that things aren't quite right. As Christians we think of that voice as the voice of God. Whispers about stress might show up in our bodies: a muscle ache, an upset stomach, or an inability to sleep, that might be telling us that we are under too much stress. Whispers sometimes show up in our emotions as moodiness, worry, or just plan crankiness. They can come as a desire to use alcohol and other drugs to calm ourselves down. Pulling away from friends and wanting to be alone can also be a whisper. God is always trying to get our attention.

If these whispers aren't listened to, they have a way of getting louder. Usually we get louder as those whispers get louder; we literally start shouting or yelling at others. We may notice ourselves being contrary and disagreeing with everyone, especially the people with whom we are close. Or we may get depressed.

If the shouts aren't heeded, our physical, emotional, relational, and/or spiritual well-being can actually fracture.

We want to learn to listen to the whispers as it is easier to do something about it when a problem is still just a whisper. It is much easier to respond to a whisper than it is to fix a fracture, as they are much more difficult to repair.

You always have a choice to respond to stress (and everything else for that matter) thoughtfully, or to merely react.

Think of a nuclear reaction. It is literally an explosion, a fracturing caused by a tremendous amount of stress on a molecular level. It takes many years for healing to occur after a nuclear explosion. When we let stress build up, when we ignore the whispers, we're headed for a nuclear explosion of our own. This type of human "nuclear" reaction can come as an emotional blow up. We will feel out of control, and blame others for our reaction. This type of explosion can also take a long time to repair. **Important relationships are frequently damaged from these types of reactions, and if we can avoid them, we should.**

There is another way to handle stress. **Instead of merely reacting, we can choose to respond thoughtfully.** When hit with stress, the person who responds is able to step out of the situation that is causing stress and take a breath or two before deciding what to do or say.

Responding thoughtfully is obviously a bit more challenging to do, but it can help us keep from adding to an already stressful situation and help us to better be able to manage the stress we can't avoid. People who are able to do this are usually people who take care of all aspects of their lives: heart, soul, strength, and mind. They work at being balanced people. **Working to better handle stress will increase your well-being and will make for a more relaxed, happy life, the kind of life God desires for you.**

Here is a list of healthy coping methods that exist in God's world that many people use to better deal with the stress in their lives. Circle some that might work for you. Can you think of others? Add them here.

- **Yoga**
- **Listening to your favorite music**
- **Talking with a friend**
- **Talking with someone who cares about you**
- **Cooking**
- **Tai Chi**
- **Getting enough sleep**
- **Engaging in a hobby that you love**
- **Playing with a pet**
- **Exercising**
- **Being organized and planning ahead**
- **Laughing**
- **Reducing caffeine intake**
- **Dancing**
- **Eating a balanced diet**
- **Singing**
- **Using healthy communication skills**

Living It

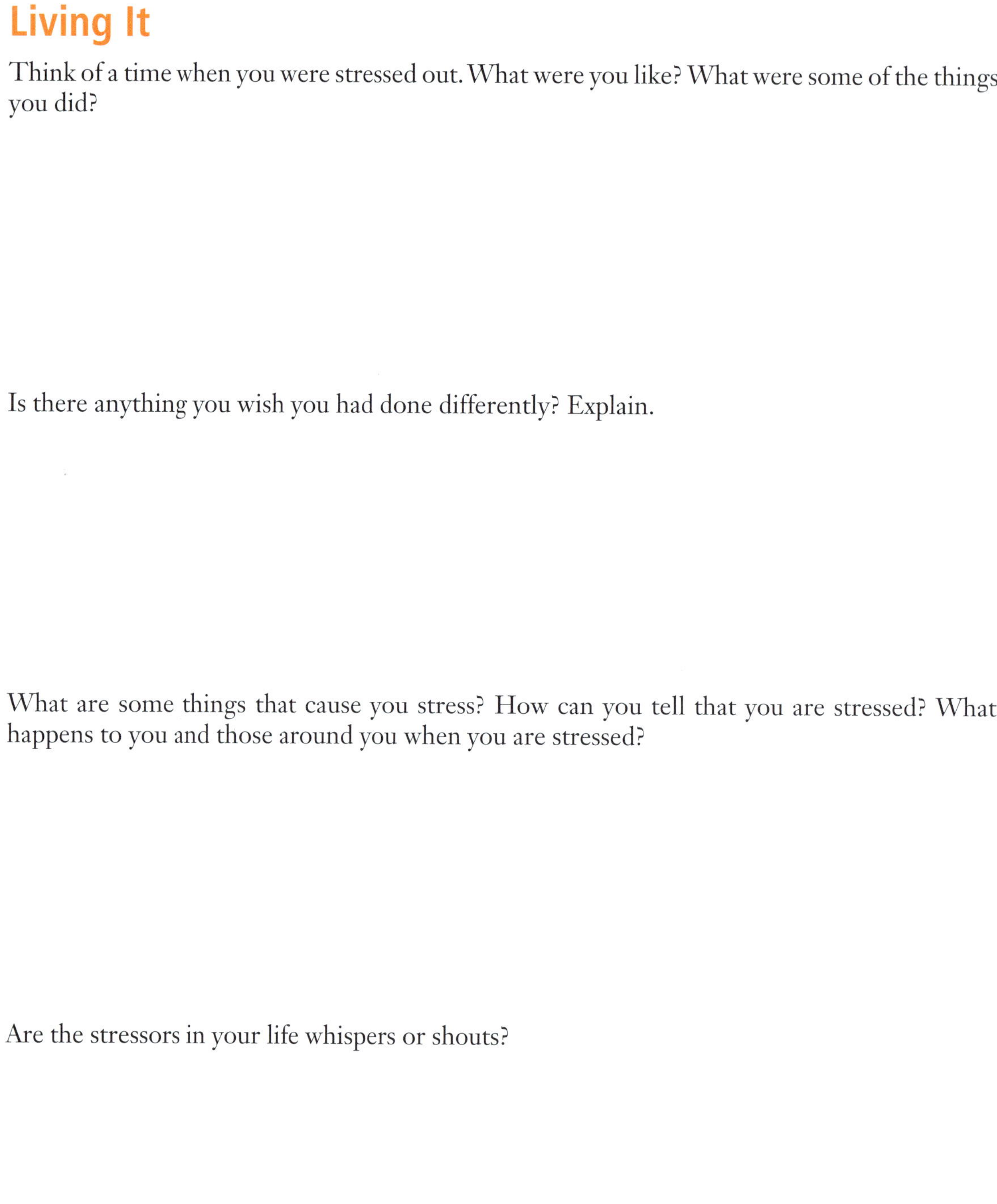

Think of a time when you were stressed out. What were you like? What were some of the things you did?

Is there anything you wish you had done differently? Explain.

What are some things that cause you stress? How can you tell that you are stressed? What happens to you and those around you when you are stressed?

Are the stressors in your life whispers or shouts?

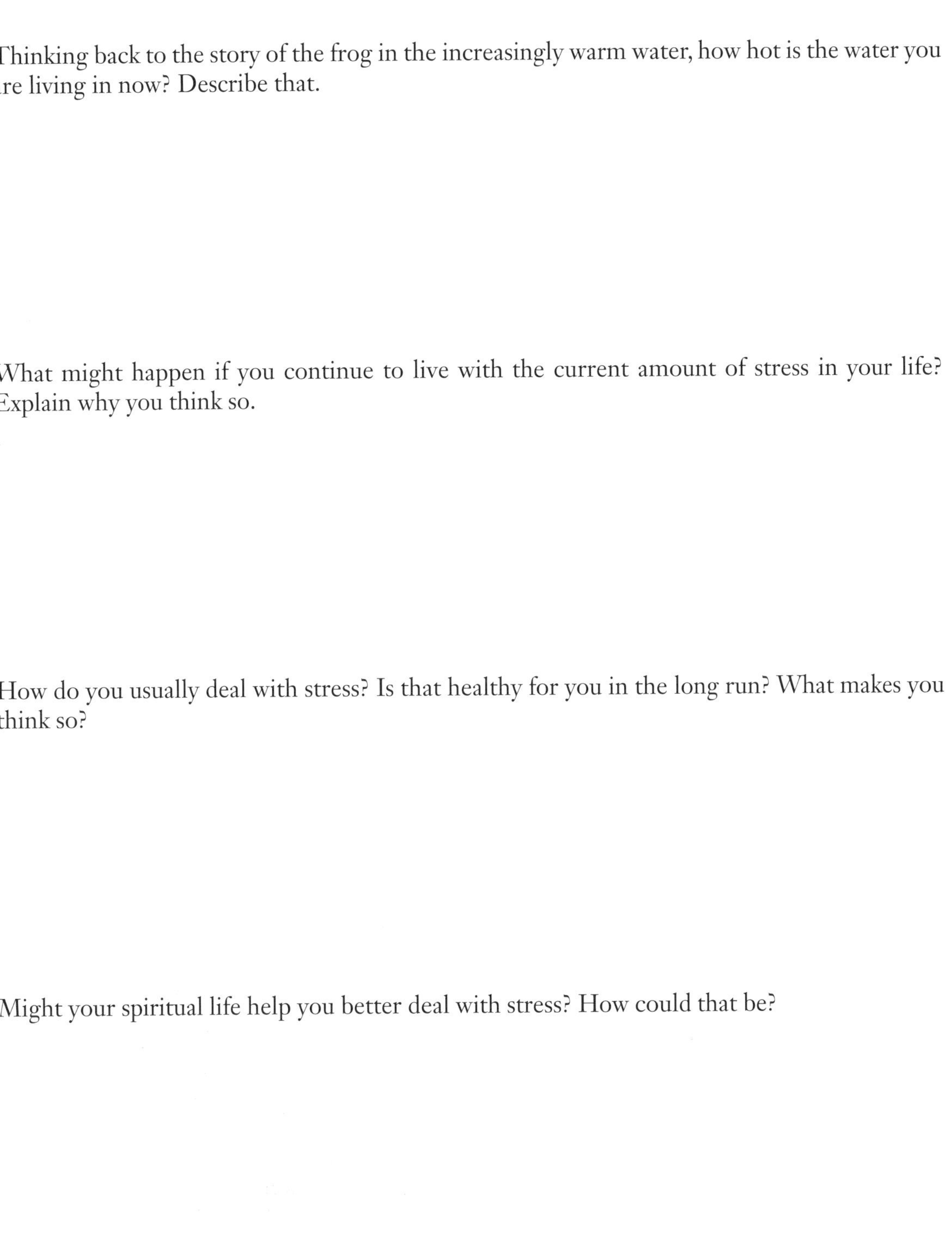

Thinking back to the story of the frog in the increasingly warm water, how hot is the water you are living in now? Describe that.

What might happen if you continue to live with the current amount of stress in your life? Explain why you think so.

How do you usually deal with stress? Is that healthy for you in the long run? What makes you think so?

Might your spiritual life help you better deal with stress? How could that be?

What calms you down? What helps you find peace? Write about it here.

Is your FAITH Step helping you to avoid, manage, or get through stress? How could you start to move in that direction? Who could help you with this? Think concretely, and be specific. Write about it here.

SECTION THREE: **Making the Connection**

> *Come to me, all you that are weary and are carrying heavy burdens, and I will give you rest. Take my yoke upon you, and learn from me; for I am gentle and humble in heart, and you will find rest for your souls. For my yoke is easy, and my burden is light.*
>
> — Matthew 11:28-30

> *Peace I leave with you; my peace I give to you. I do not give to you as the world gives. Do not let your hearts be troubled, and do not let them be afraid.*
>
> — John 14:27

Spiritual people use their faith to help them handle stress effectively, and you can condition yourself to better handle stress, as well.

How could these verses help guide you as you respond to stress?

How much of a factor is stress in the lives of teens?

How do teens usually deal with stress?

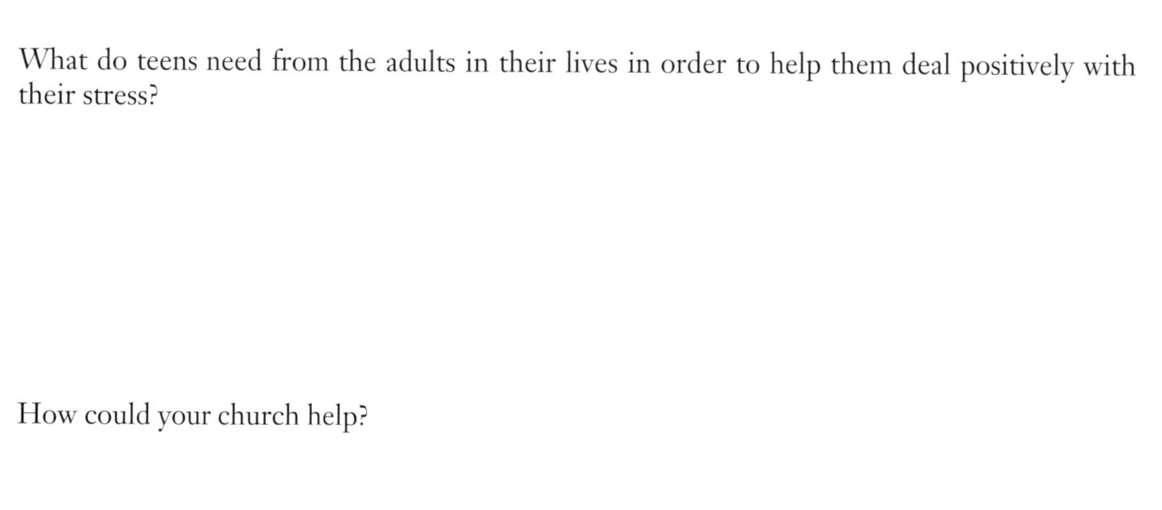

What do teens need from the adults in their lives in order to help them deal positively with their stress?

How could your church help?

In Paul's letter to the Galatians he lists nine fruits of the Spirit: love, joy, peace, patience, kindness, goodness, faithfulness, gentleness, and self-control. As you read this list, is there one you would like to focus on in your life to reduce stress? Which one and why?

Look at the answers you gave on page 22. Which score would you like to raise and why? How does this relate to Paul's words?

How would raising that number improve your life and reduce your stress? Be specific.

Who could you talk to about your stress and how could they help you?

What is one small thing you can add to your FAITH Step this week that could help you reduce your stress or deal with it more effectively?

Is there a specific prayer that might be helpful? Write it here.

STRESS IS A PART OF OUR LIVES. There is no getting away from it, but you can learn to deal with it in a healthy way.

Like all things, this takes practice, practice, practice. But, it can be done. You can do it by making good decisions and getting the support of others, including God.

Use the space below to reflect on this section. Remember: what you write is private, and nobody should see it unless you want to share it with them.

UNIT 3

Relationships

God of Kindness, sometimes it is easier for me to buy friendship than to give myself. I need to be aware that every friend of mine is a gift from you and not something to be taken for granted. Please help me to love and respect all of my friends. When the opportunity comes for me to show my love for them, help me to take advantage of that situation and do so. Help me to appreciate your unconditional love for me as the best gift of all. Today I will be caring and kind, and thank you, God, for the gift of friends in my life. Amen.

—Meaghan, age 17

SECTION ONE: Listening to Yourself

Relationships are important. Relationships are how you interact with another great gift God has given you: other people. While there are times you might feel alone, there are other people walking around the planet with you: people in your school, neighborhood, workplace, city/ town/ village, and in your home. You can build relationships with them.

Nothing affects the quality of your life like the quality of your relationships.

Think about it. A fight with a good friend can ruin a day. A word of praise from your parent or teacher can make you feel good. If a friend betrays you or a parent leaves you, it can make all the other parts of your life seem like a useless endeavor. **Relationships can give us energy or drain us of needed energy. They are very important, and we all need to be intentional about how we build them and participate in them.**

With relationships being such an important part of your life, it is important to pause and take time to look at the relationships you have right now. Please take a few moments and rate the statements on the following Self-Assessment. This assessment isn't for anyone but you; you can respond to these statements honestly. You don't need to show your answers to anyone unless you choose to. This is an opportunity for you to listen and get to know yourself.

Relationships

The ability to create and maintain healthy, life-giving connections with others.

Rate the following 10 statements from 0–10 based on the scale below, and then write your responses on the lines provided. When you are finished, add up your responses and then shade in the total score in the **Relationships** section of the Compass Self-Assessment Tool on page 3. (See pages 4 and 5 for examples.)

Never		Sometimes		Half of the Time			Most of the Time			Always
0	1	2	3	4	5	6	7	8	9	10

I am satisfied with the amount of time I spend with the important people in my life. _____

My Christian faith serves as an important guide for me in my relationships. _____

I feel good about the relationships that I have with my family members. _____

I am happy with my friendships and other social connections. _____

My friends and those who know me well would say that I am a good and trusted friend. _____

My friends and I share the same values. _____

I feel good about the impact my use/or non-use of alcohol and other drugs has on my relationships with my friends and family. _____

I feel proud of the amount of trust, respect, and honesty that exists in all of my relationships, including my dating relationships, if applicable. _____

When conflict comes up with family or friends, I am able to talk about it and resolve it in a productive way. _____

I am able to identify and end unhealthy relationships when I need to. _____

TOTAL _____

Looking carefully at the scores you gave yourself, do you see one area that could use more attention, one area that if you paid more attention to it would benefit or improve your life? Think concretely as you create a FAITH Step for yourself that you feel willing to commit to over the next several weeks. This is only for you, so make sure it is something that you really feel is important to you and fits who you are. Write your FAITH Step on the next page, and then share aloud with at least one person. List one step that is: Focused, Action Oriented, Inspired, Time Sensitive, and Heartfelt and Honest. (See pages 6 and 7 for instructions and a sample FAITH Step.)

Create a FAITH Step

Area of Wellness: Relationships

Date: ______________

Overarching Goal:
Focused: **A**ction: **I**nspired: **T**ime Sensitive: **H**eartfelt and Honest:

Obstacles:	Solutions:

Final FAITH Step:

SECTION TWO: **Learning**

There are many people who have healthy, happy, life-affirming relationships with all kinds of people: their friends, teachers, employers, parents and grandparents, and brothers and sisters. Sometimes these folks are fortunate to be in homes and neighborhoods where healthy relationships are nurtured. And some have learned from others about how to have healthy relationships, and work at it each day. Research shows that people who have healthy relationships live longer, healthier lives.

Research has also shown that being in unhealthy or unhappy relationships increases your chances of being sick by 35%. Being in unhappy relationships can also cause depression, increase the temptation to use drugs, tobacco, and/or alcohol and even lead to thoughts of suicide. Being in an unhealthy relationship can result in forming unhealthy relationship habits, which increases your risk of at some time in your life being in a relationship that is either emotionally or physically abusive. Unhealthy relationships can hurt you deeply, leaving emotional hurts that may take years to heal. Such relationships can make it difficult for you to develop other healthy relationships that are filled with love and respect, leaving you feeling "stuck." But it doesn't have to be this way.

Relationships are complicated things. They require time, energy, and skills to nurture and cultivate. Too often, it seems like relationships are something that just happen. It seems that there is very little you can do about them. **The reality is that every relationship is something that two people create over time. Each person contributes to the way the relationship works, and each person has the power to change the relationship if it is not working.**

That means YOU co-create and influence the relationships you are in, with all of the people in your life. The choices you make about how you behave in your relationships will have powerful influence on how those relationships grow or don't grow and what they, and your life, end up looking like.

Perhaps you have seen the old movie, Titanic, which portrays a romantic relationship. The movie highlights the relationship between Jack and Rose, people from two different backgrounds who share an attraction to each other. When people talk about what they loved about that movie, many say it is because the story of Jack and Rose is such a great love story. What they shared was powerful; it hit them both at a deep level, but what they had shouldn't be confused with real love.

"Falling in love," that kind of powerful attraction to another person, feels good. It is fun and enjoyable. However, that good feeling may not be enough to take two people through the challenges of life. If Jack hadn't died, he and Rose would have had to face a variety of challenges in order to build a good life together. After being together for only three days, it is impossible to tell if they could have weathered the storms of life and grown closer over time. We don't know because they did not have the opportunity to "stand in love."

When you stand in love you are willing to stand with another person no matter what happens to you, be they a family member, a friend, a love interest, or someone at school, work, or church. That means the two of you are willing to work through conflict instead of staying mad, walking away, or dropping each other completely. Standing in love means forgiving someone who hurts you and asking for their forgiveness when you hurt them. Standing in love means listening to another's ideas, feelings, and opinions. Standing in love means respecting others, not using them to get what you want. It means being curious about their point of view.

Again, standing in love isn't just for your relationship with your boyfriend or girlfriend. Standing in love is how you show love to your parents, grandparents, siblings, friends, and pretty much everyone. Standing in love means the ground you stand on in your relationships is the ground made up of values, such as trust, integrity, honesty, commitment, and kindness. That means you will act out of those values not just when you want to, but on a consistent basis.

Relationships take a lot of effort and standing in love is not easy, but if we tend to our relationships, they can be wonderful, life-giving parts of our lives.

Think about your relationships. Are they life giving and an example of how God describes love in First Corinthians?

> *Love is patient, love is kind. It does not envy, it does not boast, it is not proud. It does not dishonor others, it is not self-seeking, it is not easily angered, it keeps no record of wrongs. Love does not delight in evil but rejoices with the truth. It always protects, always trusts, always hopes, always perseveres. Love never fails.*
>
> —I Corinthians 13:4-8 (NIV)

Which of your relationships reflect these values? Which do not? Why is that? Think about family and friends. Think about how they make choices and how you make choices.

Based on what you know about these people, do you believe they share the same values you do? What makes you think so? How does that impact your relationship? How do you feel about that?

Despite what others are doing, are you doing your best to be loving toward others?

It can be challenging to have a healthy relationship with someone who does not share your basic values, so it is a good idea to find out about values early on in any relationship to avoid conflict later. Taking time to get to know someone before you get too involved with them protects you from possible trouble and hurt in the future.

Our words and our actions can affect our relationships in lots of ways. Sometimes another person will get angry because of something you have said or done. Sometimes another person will make you mad. It may be something either of you did intentionally, or something you didn't even think about. Either way, it hurts the other person, and will take effort to repair that relationship. **Your values and your Christian faith will help you determine how you live into relationships with others.**

Take a look at the following:

Feel… then Act… then Think *versus* Feel… then Think… then Act

Feel … then Act … then Think describes someone who does or says something without thinking, and the results can be hurtful. Feel … then Think … then Act describes someone who is aware that their words and actions have the potential to make their relationships better or worse. They choose carefully before they speak or do something. We all have times when we speak without thinking, which is normal. Apart from an occasional slip up, which style of communication do you think you usually use? **Circle it above.**

Write about a conversation you had with someone where *you* spoke or acted without thinking. How did the situation unfold? Tell the story here.

Think about that same conversation, but this time imagine you thought before you spoke. What might have been different? What hurt feelings or conflict might have been avoided had you tried to show the kind of care described in I Corinthians 13:4-8?

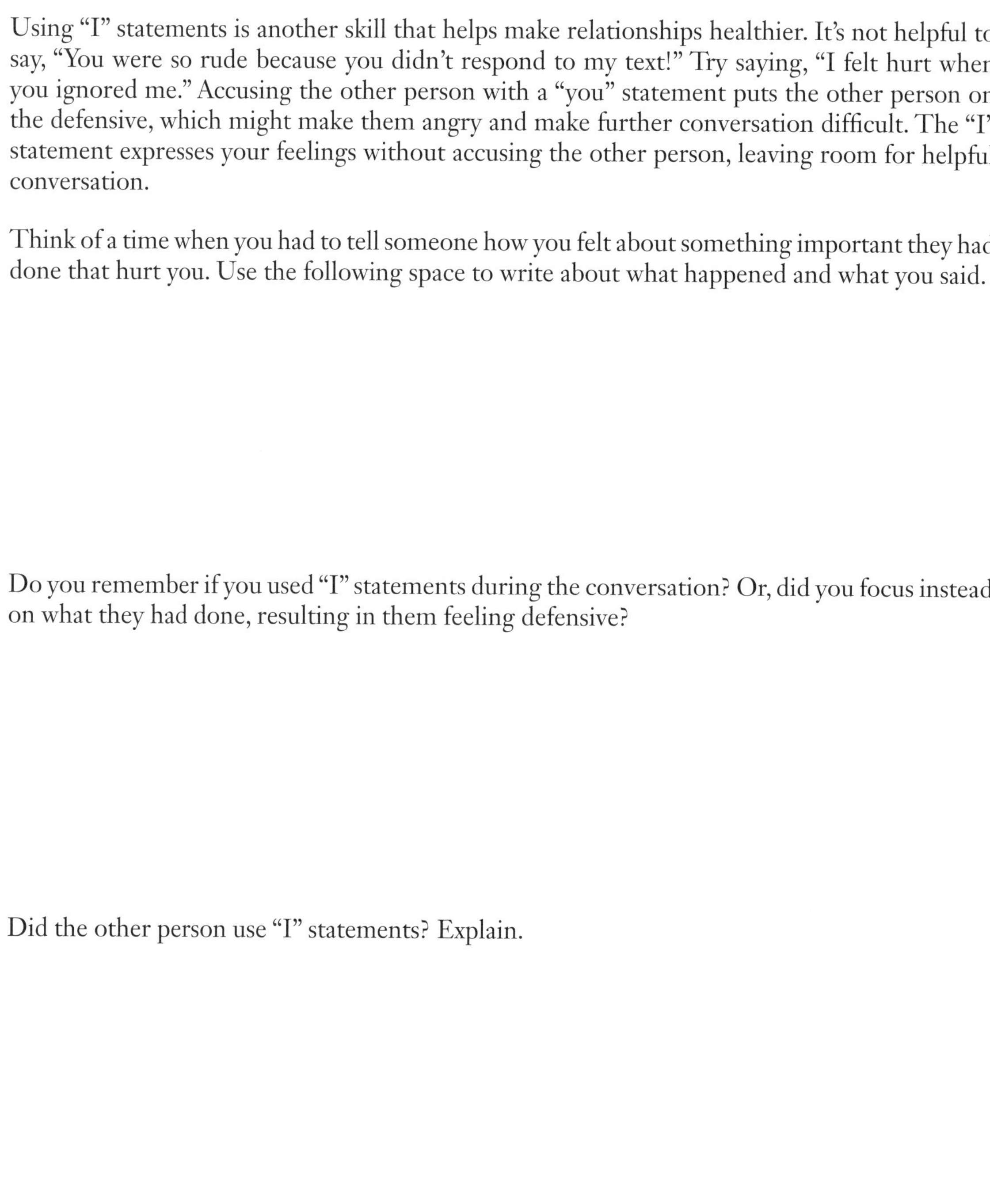

Using "I" statements is another skill that helps make relationships healthier. It's not helpful to say, "You were so rude because you didn't respond to my text!" Try saying, "I felt hurt when you ignored me." Accusing the other person with a "you" statement puts the other person on the defensive, which might make them angry and make further conversation difficult. The "I" statement expresses your feelings without accusing the other person, leaving room for helpful conversation.

Think of a time when you had to tell someone how you felt about something important they had done that hurt you. Use the following space to write about what happened and what you said.

Do you remember if you used "I" statements during the conversation? Or, did you focus instead on what they had done, resulting in them feeling defensive?

Did the other person use "I" statements? Explain.

If not, how might things have turned out better if everyone had not pointed fingers at each other and had, instead, used "I" statements?

Remember: God asks us to take responsibility for our mistakes, forgives us, and then asks us to try, with God's help, to do better in thought, word, and deed the next time. God also asks us to forgive ourselves and others.

Learning to talk through things instead of acting out feelings of hurt or frustration also helps create healthy relationships. An example of acting out your feelings would be refusing to talk to that friend who didn't respond to your text, and talking negatively behind his or her back. A more helpful option would be to talk things out instead. When you see the friend who didn't text you back, you could ask them for a few minutes alone and express your hurt and confusion at being ignored—using "I" statements, of course!

Those are really the two choices you have: to talk or to act. If you don't talk it out, if you try to ignore whatever you are feeling, chances are you are going to act out your feelings one way or another. People who study healthy relationships know that talking things out calmly is a key ingredient.

Healthy relationships are grounded in talking things out.

Write about a time you were hurt by someone. What did they do, or not do, and how did you feel? How did you let them know what you were feeling? What happened? Could using an "I" statement in the conversation with them have helped?

If you want to have a better relationship with that person going forward, what could you do differently in situations like that one?

Healthy relationships involve trust. If a relationship is healthy, each person in the relationship trusts that the other person will not betray their confidences or privacy. Trust goes two ways.

However, do not confuse trust with keeping serious secrets that involve protecting information that is harmful to you or another person. Drug or alcohol abuse, sexual misconduct of any type, criminal behavior, and physical or emotional abuse are examples of the types of secrets someone might hold. These secrets burden the keeper of the secret. If holding the confidence of one person is in any way hurting another person, you need to evaluate the need to maintain that confidence. The same is true if someone is hurting you. You must seriously consider speaking up. It may not be easy, and you will most likely need the help of a trusted adult or friend but in the end, it will lead to better health for you.

Are you keeping any secrets that are a burden to you? The secrets can be your own or those of another.

If you feel it is hurting you in any way to keep the secret, whom can you trust to help carry the burden of this secret? Who could help you deal with this issue in your life?

Are you ready to talk about your secret, if you have one? Why or why not?

Remember that there are people who can help you with any problem you might have. You just have to let the right person know that you need help. It could be a parent, grandparent, sibling, other family member, teacher, police officer, clergy person, coach, counselor, or a friend.

An important thing to consider before talking about something important with anyone you care about is to first think about what you want, what you want to say, and what you can do to get what you want. It can be frustrating, yet ultimately helpful, when dealing with people to acknowledge that you cannot change the other person; you cannot make them behave the way you want them to behave. However, what you can do is to know what you want out of the relationship, say what you want by expressing it clearly to the other person, and then working to get what you want.

Think of a relationship that you might want to improve. Maybe it is a relationship with a friend, someone at school, a sibling, or a parent. Now think about these three points as they pertain to that relationship.

Know What You Want. Identify what improvement you want to see happen. Examples might be that you want to fight less, spend more time together, be more respectful of one another, or have less teasing. Only you can identify what change you would like to make to create a healthier relationship.

Say What You Want. Think of a few versions or ways of saying to the person what you want in your relationship. An example might be, "Sam, I am glad you are my brother, but I think we are getting too old to tease each other so much. I would like for us to stop teasing as it can be hurtful sometimes."

Work to Get What You Want. Do your part to make the changes you believe will be helpful. Keep it up and be patient as change may take some time.

NOTE: If the other person does not agree with you that a change needs to be made, or if they are not willing to work with you, then chances are things won't change. Remember, you can't make another person change. What you can do is be the best person you can be, and work to get what you need. You can speak honestly about how you really feel, working at the same time to get what you need. If the relationship is hurtful, or not healthy in another way, you may need to end the relationship.

It isn't enough to talk about peace. One must believe it.
And it isn't enough to believe in it. One must work at it.
—Eleanor Roosevelt

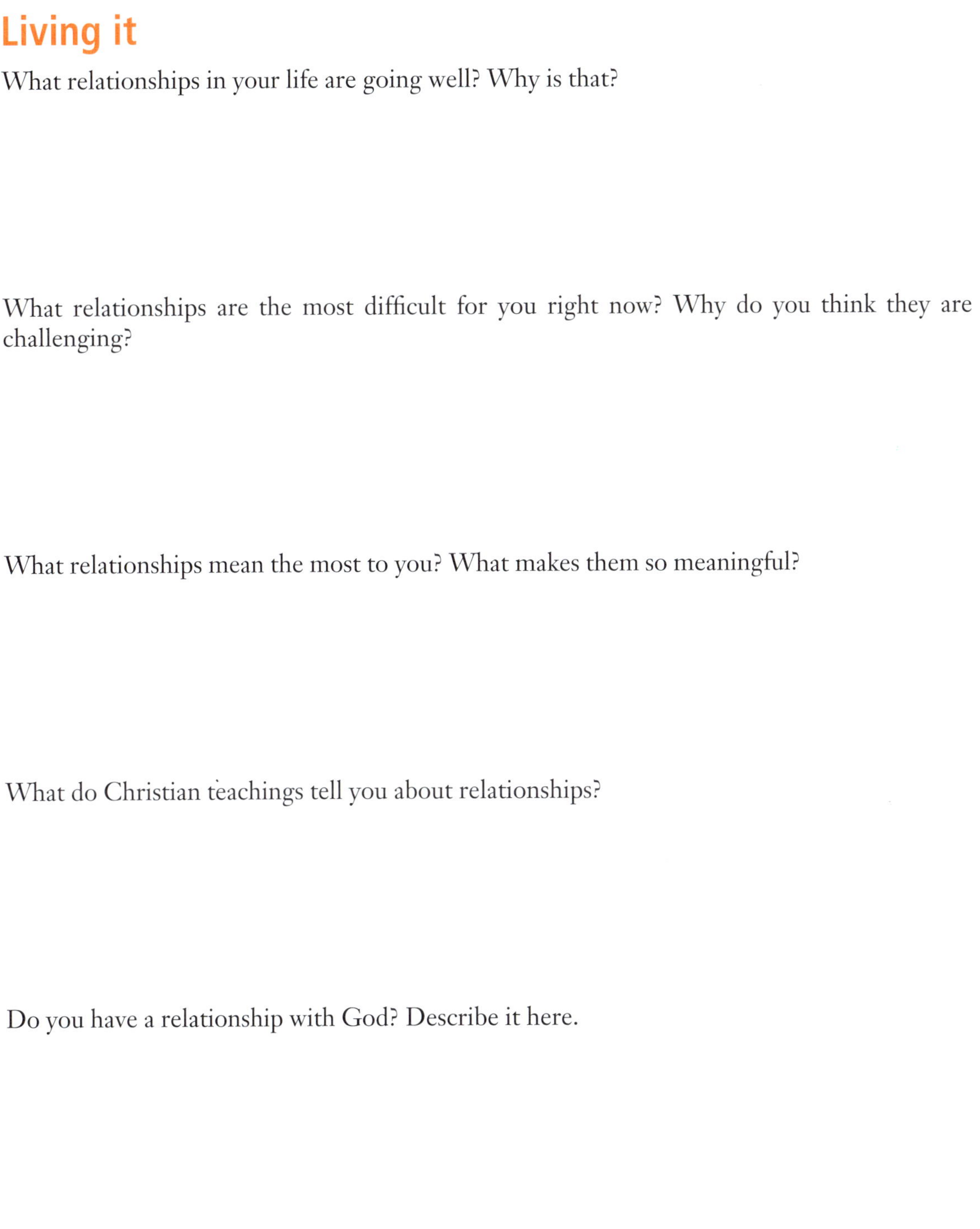

Living it

What relationships in your life are going well? Why is that?

What relationships are the most difficult for you right now? Why do you think they are challenging?

What relationships mean the most to you? What makes them so meaningful?

What do Christian teachings tell you about relationships?

Do you have a relationship with God? Describe it here.

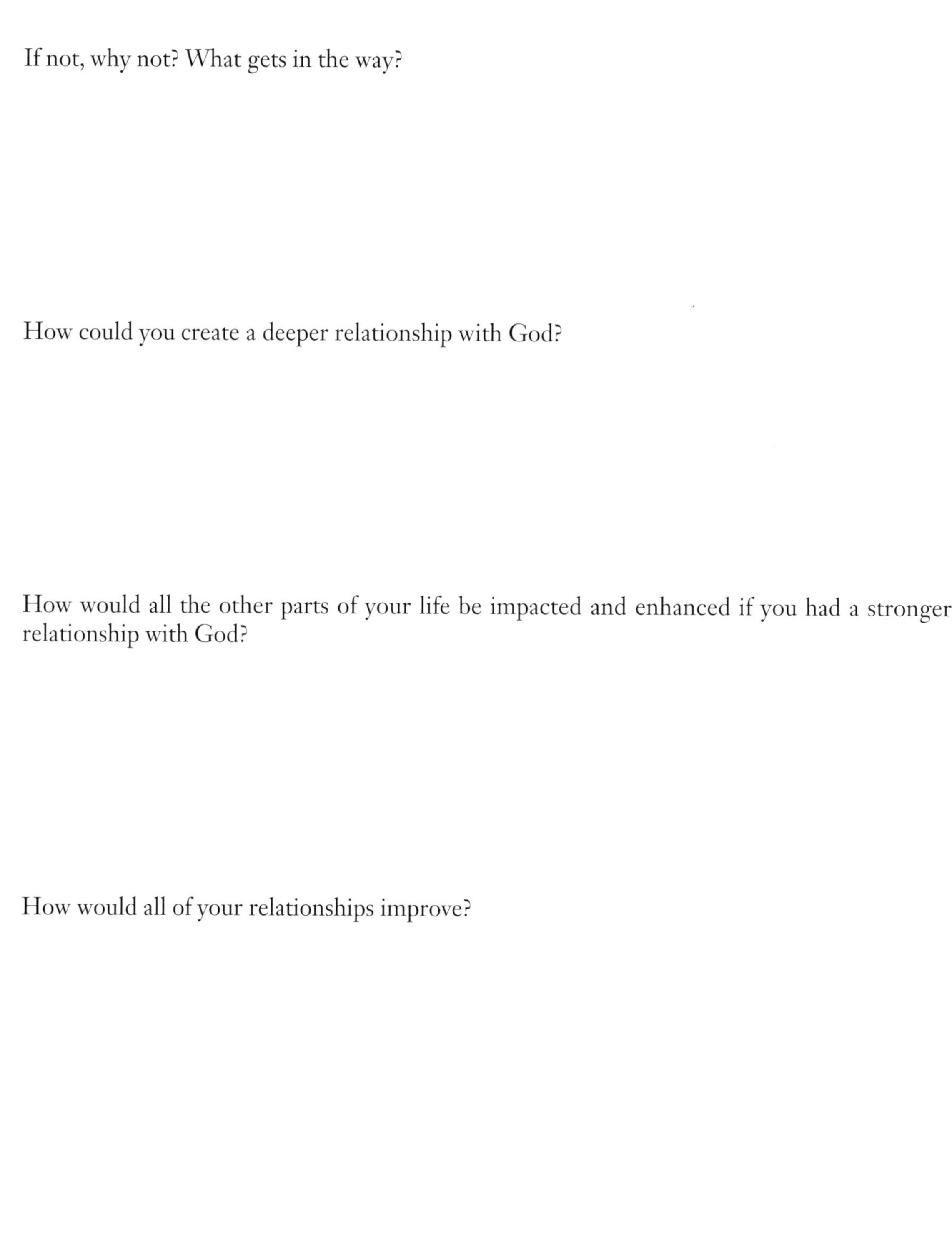

If not, why not? What gets in the way?

How could you create a deeper relationship with God?

How would all the other parts of your life be impacted and enhanced if you had a stronger relationship with God?

How would all of your relationships improve?

SECTION THREE: **Making the Connection**

You shall not hate in your heart anyone of your kin; you shall reprove your neighbor, or you will incur guilt yourself. You shall not take vengeance or bear a grudge against any of your people, but you shall love your neighbor as yourself: I am the Lord.

—Leviticus 19:17-18

Bear with one another and, if anyone has a complaint against another, forgive each other; just as the Lord has forgiven you, so you also must forgive.

—Colossians 3:13

There are six things that the Lord hates, seven that are an abomination to him: haughty eyes, a lying tongue, and hands that shed innocent blood, a heart that devises wicked plans, feet that hurry to run to evil, a lying witness who testifies falsely, and one who sows discord in a family.

—Proverbs 6:16-19

You shall not steal; you shall not deal falsely; and you shall not lie to one another.

—Leviticus 19:11

How might the wisdom of these verses help you in your current relationships?

Forgiving, honoring, being honest, and loving others are hard work for all of us, yet are important if we want to build life-giving relationships. How is it challenging to live the way the Bible suggests as a teen in today's world? Site examples. Be specific about how living by these guidelines are challenging.

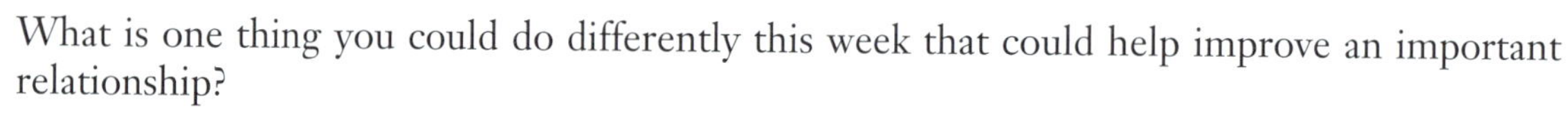

What is one thing you could do differently this week that could help improve an important relationship?

What would be a good way to start to make that change? Be concrete.

Do you need to talk to someone else to help make this happen? Who would this be and how could they help?

How would improving this relationship make your life better and perhaps more in line with what God wants for you and others?

Review your FAITH Step on page 34. Has the FAITH Step you have been working on helped to improve an important relationship? Be specific about that relationship and what you could do to improve it.

But I say unto you, love your enemies, bless them that curse you, do good to them that hate you, and pray for them which despitefully use you, and persecute you.

—Matthew 5:44

Remember, you co-create the relationships you are in. You can make a difference.

Use the space below to reflect on this section. Remember: what you write is private, and nobody should see it unless you want to share it with them.

UNIT 4

Rest and Play

God of Laughter, I need your strength. Right now I am stressed; I'm pulled in too many directions. My boss wants me to work, my coach wants me to practice, I need to do homework, and yet I want to be with my friends. I feel so weak, like putty pulled and stretched. Some days I wake up and wonder, is this all there is to life? People tell me that you, God, are watching over me all the time. I believe that. Take stress from me today and help me begin with a fresh new view, one that is more peaceful and less stressful. Help me realize that life is beautiful and needs to be fun. There is resurrection. Today I will take a time-out, if only for a few minutes, and do something fun: look through some old pictures, do something silly—anything to help me be more aware of the joy of today. Amen.

—Jason, age 16

SECTION ONE: Listening to Yourself

The opening prayer says it all! There are times when you feel pulled in many different directions, all at once. Everyone wants a piece of you, and all of those people are important. Yes, there is a lot that needs to be done and many demands are placed on you as a teen. Your life doesn't have to be crazy and out of control, though. The most important things can get done, and YOU can do them and do them well, especially when you take time for rest and play. Rest and play are an important part of caring for yourself as they help give you the energy you need for the rest of your life. You, just like your phone, need recharging on a regular basis.

Take a few minutes and rate the statements on the following Rest and Play Self-Assessment. These questions are just for you; no one else needs to see how you score yourself unless you want to share your answers with someone else. This is a way for you to pause, to take a break from listening to all the voices telling you what to do and to listen to yourself, and to that quiet whisper within you that is God. What you do with your answers is up to you. Answer each question honestly for the most helpful results.

Rest and Play

The ability to balance work and play and to renew one's self.

Rate the following 10 statements from 0–10 based on the scale below, and then write your responses on the lines provided. When you are finished, add up your responses and then shade in the total score in the **Rest and Play** section of the Compass Self-Assessment Tool on page 3. (See pages 4 and 5 for examples.)

Never		Sometimes		Half of the Time			Most of the Time			Always
0	1	2	3	4	5	6	7	8	9	10

I get enough rest to rejuvenate myself most of the time. _____

I am satisfied with the amount of time that I have set aside for healthy fun. _____

I have at least one hobby or interest that renews me, and I take intentional time for it on a regular basis. _____

I feel good about the kinds of activities I do during my free time, and know they are good for my overall well-being. _____

I enjoy my recreational involvement in activities at school, at church, or with other local organizations. _____

I actively take advantage of opportunities to try new activities and new ways to have fun. _____

I am confident that my connection to technology, such as video games, TV, computer, social media, and cell phone, is good for my overall well-being. _____

I frequently have fun where alcohol and other drugs are not present. _____

The people with whom I spend my free time are a good influence on me. _____

I use some of my free time as Sabbath time to renew my spirituality. _____

TOTAL _____

Looking carefully at the scores you gave yourself, do you see one area that could use more attention, one area that if you paid more attention to it would benefit or improve your life? Think concretely as you create a FAITH Step for yourself that you feel willing to commit to over the next several weeks. This is only for you, so make sure it is something that you really feel is important to you and fits who you are. Write your FAITH Step on the next page, and then share aloud with at least one person. List one step that is: Focused, Action Oriented, Inspired, Time Sensitive, and Heartfelt and Honest. (See pages 6 and 7 for instructions and a sample FAITH Step.)

Create a FAITH Step

Area of Wellness: Rest and Play

Date: ______

Overarching Goal:	
Focused:	
Action:	
Inspired:	
Time Sensitive:	
Heartfelt and Honest:	
Obstacles:	Solutions:
Final FAITH Step:	

SECTION TWO: **Learning**

Have you ever been talking or texting on your phone when, right in the middle of your conversation, your phone dies? That can be really frustrating. It can be even worse if you are lost and trying to let someone know where you are or are trying to get directions. When you look to see why the call failed and discover that the battery is dead, the frustration worsens. There is nothing wrong with your phone; it isn't broken. You aren't out of range. Your phone can't work because you did not charge the battery.

IT IS IMPORTANT TO KEEP *YOUR* BATTERY CHARGED!

Just like our devices, we each have a sort of internal battery that needs to be plugged in to the right source so we can get recharged. Right now you have a personal battery that is running on a charge, and only you know if you have a full charge, a half charge, less than half, or are almost out of power.

How much charge do you have these days?

While there inevitably will be times when we are less than fully charged than others, we know that we all operate better when we are fully charged, meaning we are full of energy. When our charge is high, we feel vibrant, healthy, and alive. To feel that way, we each need to find our own unique ways to keep our batteries charged and that comes from our rest and play.

One of the ways we get our batteries charged is by participating in some form of recreation. Many people think of watching TV or spending time on a computer as recreation, and it can be. On the other hand, it isn't necessarily recreation; in fact, doing something passively for too long can leave us drained of energy. You will have a better chance of truly recharging your batteries when you make intentional choices about the activities that help to renew *your* heart, soul, mind, and body.

Allowing time for rest on a regular basis means more than not working. It means taking a break from your regular activities in order to create time for you. It means unplugging from all the chatter that is constantly streaming at you from television, social media, gossip from your friends, the music you listen to—all of it. Having room for Sabbath time, originally suggested by religious communities but now adopted by people everywhere, means setting aside the everyday responsibilities of life and connecting with God. For you this could mean taking a break from Facebook for a day and instead sitting down and talking with someone you care about and who cares about you. It could mean taking a break to spend some time on a hobby you enjoy, or taking a hike or bike ride, or some other physical activity you enjoy doing. Think about those things that excite and inspire you. Perhaps you love reading, writing, painting, drawing, or working with clay. Maybe playing music or singing does it for you, or working in a garden, or cooking, reading, or playing a sport. Only you know what excites you, what makes you happy, what recharges your batteries. It's different for everyone.

Typically, a person's strength is thought of as being something at which they excel. You are sometimes encouraged to examine your strengths as a means to focus on potential career opportunities. However, a strength can also be seen as something that gives you energy, even if you do not excel at it. Using this definition, if dancing gives you energy and lightens your life, then dancing is a strength for you, even if you lack rhythm or style. On the other hand, if you excel at playing the piano but take no pleasure in it, playing the piano is not truly one of your strengths. What are your strengths? What gives you energy?

Sabbath means taking intentional time to connect with God.

Just as there are things that renew your energy and make you feel alive, connected with God and your soul, there are things that can have the opposite effect. These are things that drain energy from you, such as a challenging subject in school, being overly committed, or dealing with a difficult situation or person. These situations and relationships are part of life, and you need to be intentional about your decisions and about how you handle them. If you do not set good boundaries with people who drain you, they will gradually take a toll on you. If you do too much, you will find your batteries drained, and you won't be able to be your best, most healthy self. If you don't take time for personal time with God, you may end up feeling depleted and alone.

It is good to be aware that some people and some activities wear you down faster than others. Being aware helps you set good boundaries so you can deal with those things or people in a healthy way.

When your battery is charged, you will feel good. You will find you have energy for all sorts of people, activities, and opportunities. You will be stronger. You will be able to pay better attention, learn faster, listen better, have more to give the world, and maybe even laugh more. You will see positive results in all areas of your life.

Living it

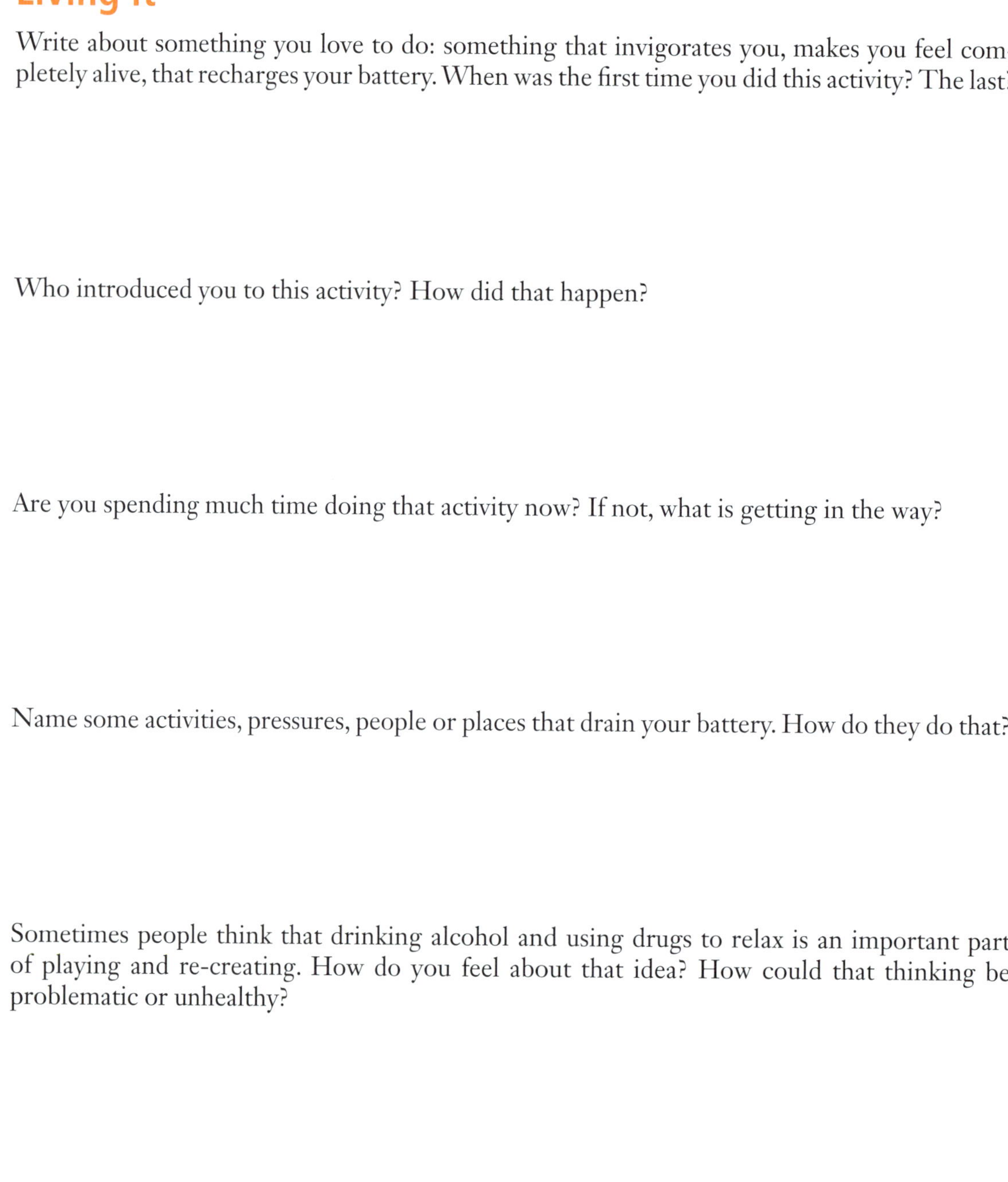

Write about something you love to do: something that invigorates you, makes you feel completely alive, that recharges your battery. When was the first time you did this activity? The last?

Who introduced you to this activity? How did that happen?

Are you spending much time doing that activity now? If not, what is getting in the way?

Name some activities, pressures, people or places that drain your battery. How do they do that?

Sometimes people think that drinking alcohol and using drugs to relax is an important part of playing and re-creating. How do you feel about that idea? How could that thinking be problematic or unhealthy?

Sometimes when we are going through a change, like starting a new school year, breaking off a significant relationship, moving to a new neighborhood, or adjusting to a significant change in the family—a death or divorce, for example—our battery can become drained pretty quickly. **All transitions, even those we have chosen and we are happy about, can drain our battery as they take much of our mental energy.**

Have you had a major change in your life? What is it?

Did you choose it or did it just happen to you? How it is going for you? Explain.

What could you do to help yourself deal with it? Think about all eight areas of wellness.

What decisions might you make going forward that could lessen the drain on your battery? Be specific.

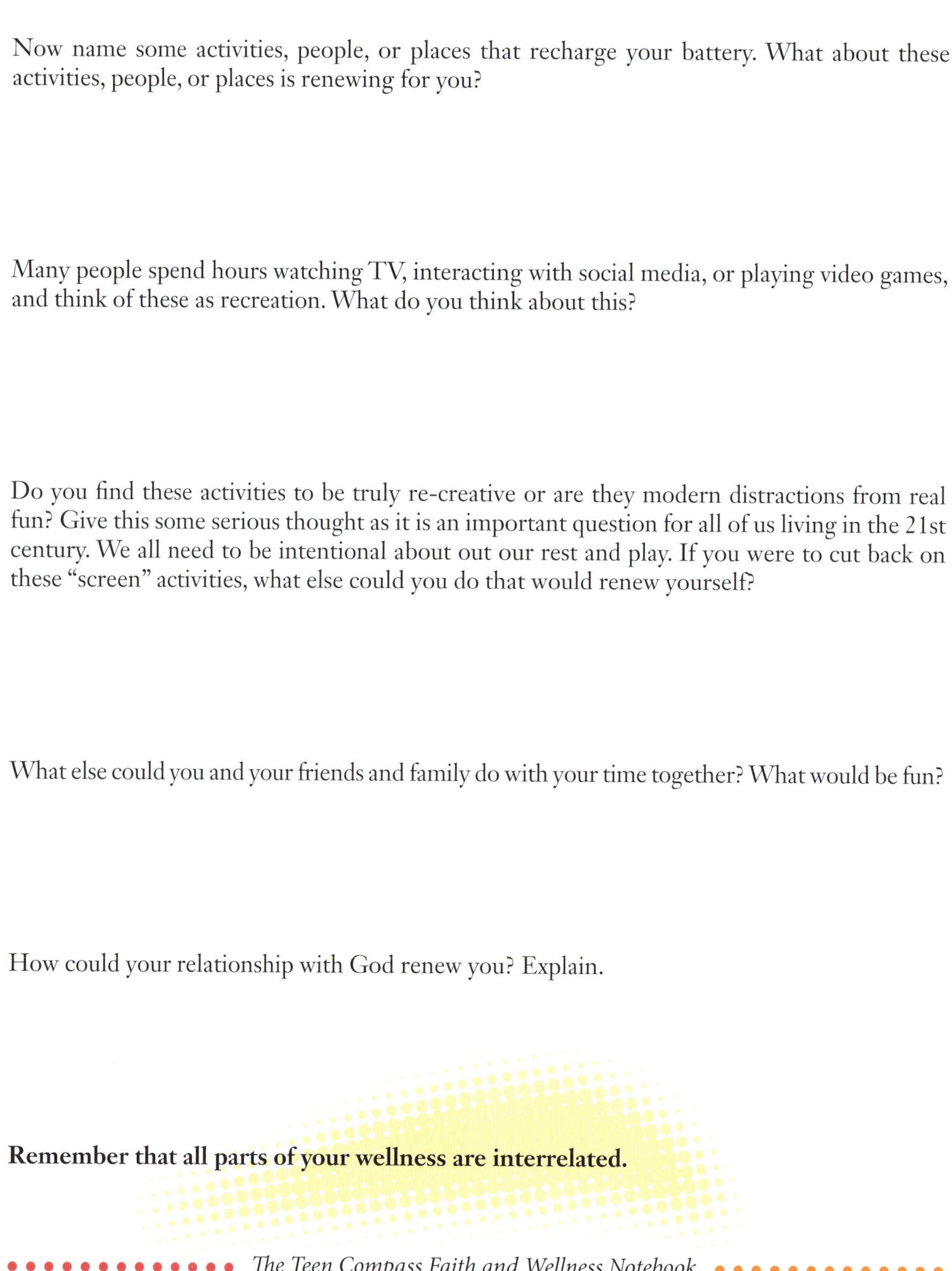

Now name some activities, people, or places that recharge your battery. What about these activities, people, or places is renewing for you?

Many people spend hours watching TV, interacting with social media, or playing video games, and think of these as recreation. What do you think about this?

Do you find these activities to be truly re-creative or are they modern distractions from real fun? Give this some serious thought as it is an important question for all of us living in the 21st century. We all need to be intentional about out our rest and play. If you were to cut back on these "screen" activities, what else could you do that would renew yourself?

What else could you and your friends and family do with your time together? What would be fun?

How could your relationship with God renew you? Explain.

Remember that all parts of your wellness are interrelated.

SECTION THREE: Making the Connection

Six days you shall work, but on the seventh day you shall rest; even in plowing time and in harvest time you shall rest.

—Exodus 34:21

Come to me, all you that are weary and are carrying heavy burdens, and I will give you rest. Take my yoke upon you, and learn from me; for I am gentle and humble in heart, and you will find rest for your souls. For my yoke is easy, and my burden is light.

—Matthew 11:28-30

He said to them, "Come away to a deserted place all by yourselves and rest a while." For many were coming and going, and they had no leisure even to eat.

—Mark 6:31

From the very beginning God had been telling us to rest, to take time for Sabbath every week. Why is this difficult in the modern world? Why do you think rest is so important?

Matthew speaks about "rest for your souls." What does this mean to you? How can you get this type of rest?

What other thoughts do you have about the wisdom of these verses and how they relate to your life right now?

Go back to your Rest and Play Self-Assessment on page 52, and look at the scores. Remember that this is your tool, and no one needs to see it unless you want to show it to someone.

Has your commitment to your FAITH Step helped to move that score a little higher?

Is there a response you gave that you feel really good about? How were you able to achieve that high score? Be specific.

Is there another statement that seems important and you would like to be able to rate higher than you did? Which one? And why does that statement seem important to you?

What is one thing, a small thing, something you know you can do that would help you feel more rested?

Do you need help doing this? Who can you ask to help you?

What might you need to take a break from in order to more fully feel God's peace?

Consider taking a Sabbath of your own—which means taking a break for a set period of time from an activity you now do—in hopes of using that time more intentionally to recharge your battery.

Maybe your Sabbath could be taking one afternoon off from the normal things you do in order to be with someone you care about, or to read a book. You might write in a journal, listen to music, do something outside, pray, or go for a run. What Sabbath activity renews you? The choice is yours!

Use the space below to reflect on this section. Remember: what you write is private, and nobody should see it unless you want to share it with them.

UNIT 5

Handling Emotions

God, give me grace to accept with serenity the things that cannot be changed, courage to change the things that should be changed, and the wisdom to distinguish the one from the other. Amen.

—Reinhold Niebuhr

SECTION ONE: **Listening to Yourself**

On an episode of *The Colbert Report with Stephen Colbert*, Colbert was interviewing a well-known actor. He asked the actor if he was able to really feel emotions or if he only knew how to pretend to have emotions. He was wondering, he explained, because as an actor it was his job to fake emotions. Colbert then noted that we will pay a lot of money to watch people on a screen or stage pretend to show certain emotions rather than express our own emotions. The observation was meant to be funny, but what made it memorable was that, in some ways, it was true. Many of us, not just actors, express emotions that are not what we are really feeling deep inside.

When you were a child, you freely expressed your emotions. When you were angry, you were angry and showed it. When you were sad, you showed that, too. When you were happy, you freely expressed it. As you grew older you began to learn the art of handling emotions in socially acceptable ways. You may have learned that it was no longer okay to show your anger, sadness, or even your happiness in the same way you used to. Learning how to handle all of these emotions is a good thing. Unfortunately, however, some folks have become concerned about expressing emotions in an inappropriate way and now, as a result, don't share many of their emotions with others. They try to hide the difficult emotions they are feeling.

What is important to remember is that God created all of our emotions as guides to help us understand the world around us. If our emotions are positive, that signals to us that things are going well. If they are uncomfortable, that means something is not right and a change is needed. All of our emotions are neither good nor bad in and of themselves. What is good or bad is how we express them, and what we do with them.

Handling and expressing all of our emotions isn't easy for anyone, but it is an essential skill to develop as we grow into adulthood. That is why we are now going to focus on handling emotions.

Take a few moments to pause and listen to yourself and reflect on how you express your emotions by taking the following Emotions Self-Assessment. Remember, this is just for you; no one else is going to see this unless you choose to share it.

Handling Emotions

The ability to express your emotions and to receive others' emotions in a healthy way.

Rate the following 10 statements from 0–10 based on the scale below, and then write your responses on the lines provided. When you are finished, add up your responses and then shade in the total score in the **Handling Emotions** section of the Compass Self-Assessment Tool on page 3. (See pages 4 and 5 for examples.)

Never		Sometimes		Half of the Time			Most of the Time			Always
0	1	2	3	4	5	6	7	8	9	10

People who know me would say I handle my emotions in a healthy way. _____

I avoid using alcohol, other drugs, and other possibly addictive behaviors to deal with my emotions. _____

The way I show my emotions demonstrates respect toward myself and others. _____

I feel good about the way I handle my emotions and how that affects my relationships. _____

I have a solid and healthy sense of confidence in myself. _____

I know the early warning signs of depression or anxiety and would feel comfortable seeking help from a trusted person if I felt this way. _____

I am able to share my full range of emotions (including sadness, happiness, fear, and worry) with people I trust. _____

I am able to communicate my emotions in a positive way without being irritable, critical, or angry. _____

When someone I care about is upset, I am comfortable listening and really being present to them. _____

When I am feeling emotionally overwhelmed, I turn to God and prayer to re-center myself. _____

TOTAL _____

Looking carefully at the scores you gave yourself, do you see one area that could use more attention, one area that if you paid more attention to it would benefit or improve your life? Think concretely as you create a FAITH Step for yourself that you feel willing to commit to over the next several weeks. This is only for you, so make sure it is something that you really feel is important to you and fits who you are. Write your FAITH Step on the next page, and then share aloud with at least one person. List one step that is: Focused, Action Oriented, Inspired, Time Sensitive, and Heartfelt and Honest. (See pages 6 and 7 for instructions and a sample FAITH Step.)

Create a FAITH Step

Area of Wellness: Handling Emotions

Date: ______

Overarching Goal:

Focused:

Action:

Inspired:

Time Sensitive:

Heartfelt and Honest:

Obstacles:	Solutions:

Final FAITH Step:

SECTION TWO: **Learning**

We all have a wide range of emotions that we feel at different times in our lives. They are all natural and normal and we may feel many of them in the course of a single day. Circle the ones that best describe how you have been feeling recently.

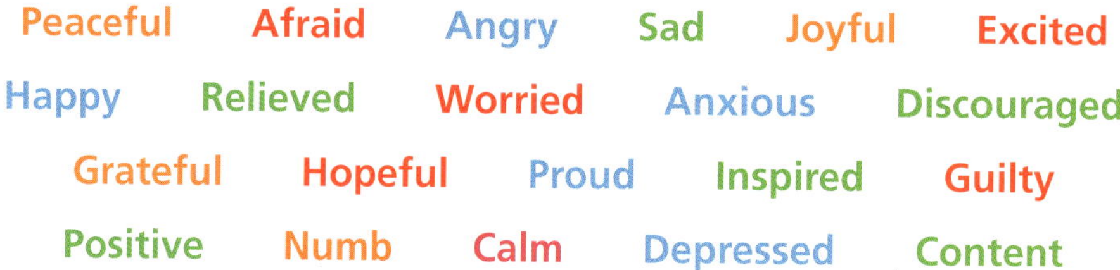

Do you feel other emotions? List them here.

Write a little bit about why you are feeling these emotions. What is going on?

How would others know you are feeling this way? Are you smiling a lot? Do you start crying easily?

Are you peaceful and relaxed? Are you overly apologetic? Are you having trouble sleeping? Are you cranky, sensitive, or argumentative? Write a bit about how you are expressing those emotions.

Do you feel that the way you are expressing your emotions is healthy? If not, what might you do to change that?

Perhaps you know people who are ruled by their emotions. Maybe you are one of them. When they are sad, they are really sad: crying, saying sad or hopeless things, being quiet, or pulling away. When they are angry you know to watch out because they'll yell, have blow-ups, and maybe even punch a locker or wall. There is no doubt about how they are feeling. The good news is that emotions are like the ocean—any of us can be swept up in the waves and be tossed about, or we can learn to swim. We can learn how to swim through our emotions so we don't drown in them.

You also most likely know others who are able to handle their emotions in a calmer way. They still feel things, and you can tell when they are happy, sad, or angry, but they don't show their emotions in a way that is scary or dangerous. Their emotions don't get in the way of their thinking, nor do they try to force you to share their feelings. These people will tell you that they are feeling sad and show it in ways that are authentic and inviting. These people will certainly get angry, but they won't frighten others when they express their anger. They are in control of their emotions rather than having their emotions control them. That is an important distinction.

In the movie *Inside Out*, there was a depiction of how, for many of us, one emotion can overtake the others if we are not careful. As this movie points out, it is important to pay attention to our emotions. They are whispers from God that a change is needed.

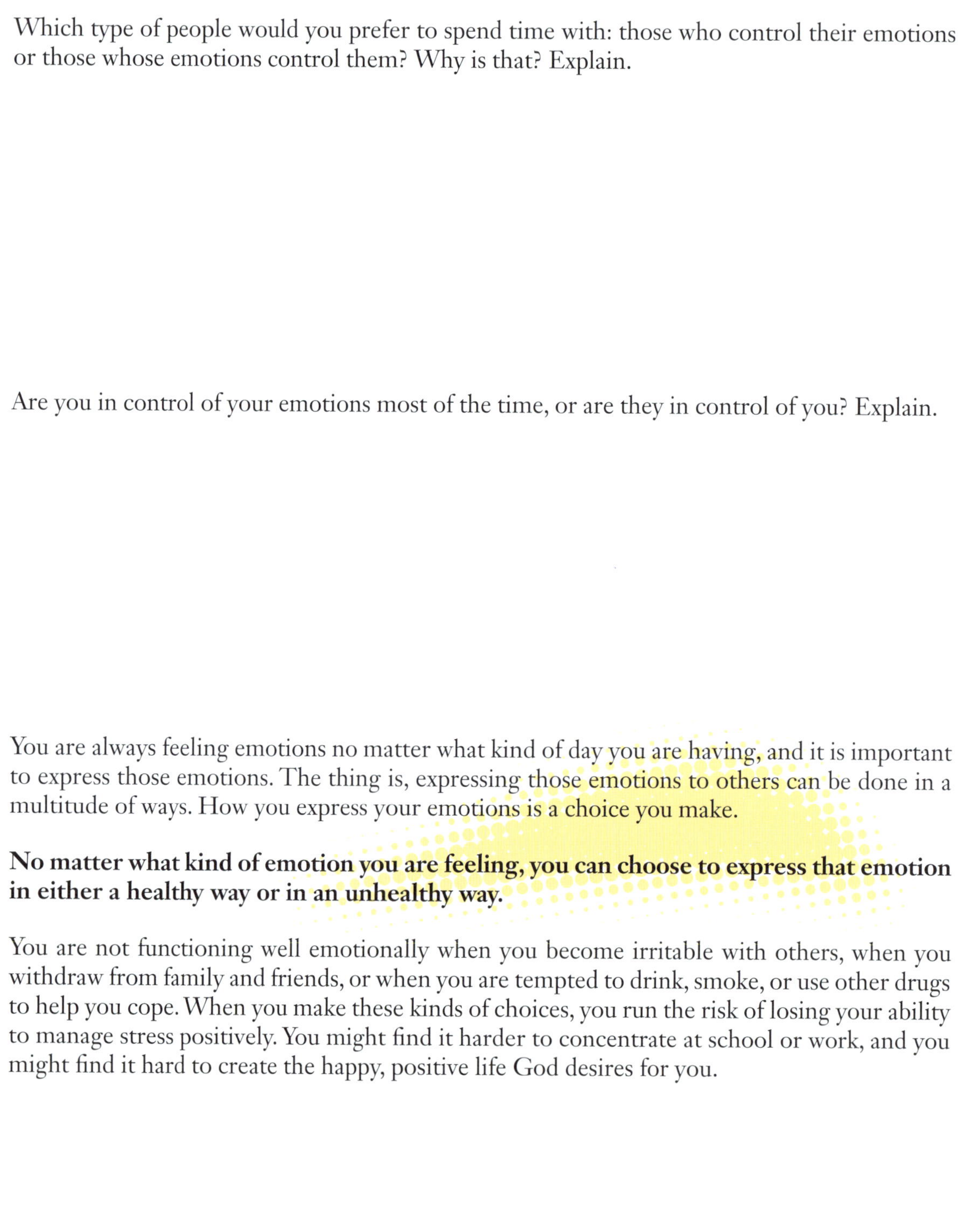

Which type of people would you prefer to spend time with: those who control their emotions or those whose emotions control them? Why is that? Explain.

Are you in control of your emotions most of the time, or are they in control of you? Explain.

You are always feeling emotions no matter what kind of day you are having, and it is important to express those emotions. The thing is, expressing those emotions to others can be done in a multitude of ways. How you express your emotions is a choice you make.

No matter what kind of emotion you are feeling, you can choose to express that emotion in either a healthy way or in an unhealthy way.

You are not functioning well emotionally when you become irritable with others, when you withdraw from family and friends, or when you are tempted to drink, smoke, or use other drugs to help you cope. When you make these kinds of choices, you run the risk of losing your ability to manage stress positively. You might find it harder to concentrate at school or work, and you might find it hard to create the happy, positive life God desires for you.

You are functioning well emotionally when you can do the following:

- Feel and express the full range of emotions in a healthy manner.
- Adapt to change fairly easily.
- Recognize the signs that your emotions are getting the better of you, such as being quick to cry or get angry.
- Make choices about how to handle your emotions.
- Have a sense of humor, a positive outlook on life, and don't take yourself too seriously.
- Intentionally choose a response to any given situation rather than merely reacting.
- Respond thoughtfully to statements, questions, circumstances, and events that happen around you.
- Talk to others about how you are feeling.

You will find that these things are not always easy to do, but you can do them more easily when you are also sleeping well, exercising, eating right, and tending to your spiritual life. One of the first indications or whispers that an area of your life is out of balance may be a change in the way you normally handle your emotions.

If you do notice a change, pay attention to what has been happening around you and how you have reacted. Take time to examine what is going on and look at areas of your life that may be in need of more attention. Use it as an opportunity to grow and … be gentle with yourself; we all have challenging days.

One time when your emotions will naturally be more difficult to handle is when you are going through a transition in your life.

Below are some transitions faced by people your age.

- Parents breaking up
- Starting at a new school
- Getting your first job
- A family member or friend becoming sick or dying
- Coming out
- An important friendship ending
- A parent remarrying
- Getting a stepparent and maybe even new step-siblings
- Beginning an important new friendship or romantic relationship
- Ending a relationship
- Moving to a new community

These are times when you will feel strong emotions, and they can be hard to manage. The support of others will help you move through these times of transition. Think of people you can talk to, confide in, and trust to listen to you: a parent, a friend, teacher, coach, grandparent, aunt or uncle, sibling, and/or clergy person.

You might be tempted to pull away from others, but don't let that happen. Don't be afraid to reach out and stay connected with others who are comfortable with what you are feeling. Remember that together we can do more than we can by ourselves. During this process of opening up you may learn better listening skills yourself and become better equipped to be a support for someone else going through a difficult time later on down the road.

Like your body, your emotions are a tremendous gift to you from God. Your emotions allow you to experience life on a deeper, more vital level. When handled poorly, emotions can hurt your life, damaging your physical health, relationships, and overall well-being. When handled well, emotions can deeply enhance relationships and help open the doors to new opportunities in life.

Singer songwriter Kirk Franklin wrote a song—*Hello Fear*—about his faith helping him find a new emotion, one he experiences as more life-giving than the fear that had been controlling him. He decides to live into that new emotion after a difficult breakup. Through the song, he is sharing what he has learned: that with much practice and intention, we can choose what emotions will be primary for us. You can download the song on iTunes, listen to it online, or on Kirk Franklin's album by the same name, *Hello Fear*.

Think of a negative emotion you are dealing with right now. Maybe it is fear, anxiety, guilt, or anger. Whatever emotion it is, you want to be able to manage it instead of having that emotion manage you. Facing it and praying about it is the beginning of making peace with it. Write about it here.

Living it

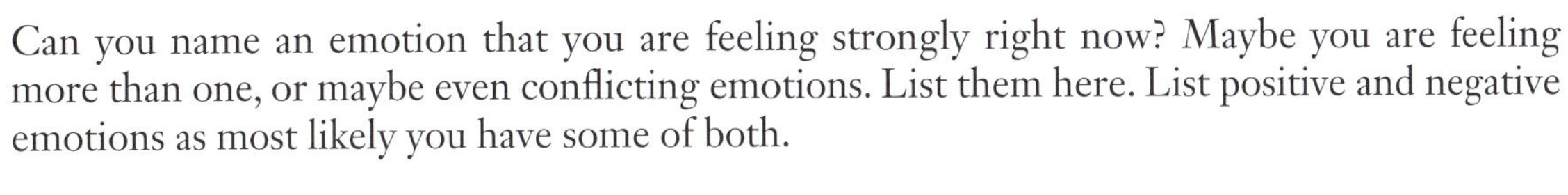

Can you name an emotion that you are feeling strongly right now? Maybe you are feeling more than one, or maybe even conflicting emotions. List them here. List positive and negative emotions as most likely you have some of both.

Maybe you feeling proud about something you have accomplished, or excited about something you are planning. Maybe you have experienced a hurt that needs to be dealt with, maybe you are going through a transition that is challenging. Write about why you think you are feeling the ways you are currently feeling. What's going on?

Do you have a difficult emotion that you are dealing with at this point? Maybe it is fear, worry, guilt, or anger. You want to be able to manage that feeling instead of having that emotion manage you. Recognizing it is the first step toward dealing with or making peace with whatever is stirring up that emotion.

Handling emotions positively is something you can do! One way is to stop and think about what you want to say, rather than blurting out something you might regret later. Remember: feel, then think, then act.

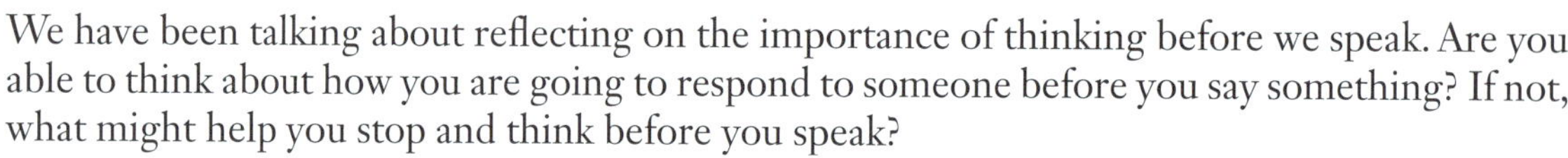
We have been talking about reflecting on the importance of thinking before we speak. Are you able to think about how you are going to respond to someone before you say something? If not, what might help you stop and think before you speak?

What kind of emotional expression do you see in books, on TV, in movies? Describe them. Are they healthy or unhealthy? How can you tell? Give some examples.

Do you feel like you have opportunities to express whatever emotions you are feeling in your life right now? Why or why not? Could you create opportunities to do so?

Think of someone you know who handles their emotions well. Who is that person? How is that person able to stay calm and centered?

What about this person would you like to imitate?

Jesus teaches us how we should handle ourselves in relationship with others. What words come to mind when thinking about Jesus's teachings regarding relating to others? Write them here.

What does emotional well-being have to do with our brains? The answer is a lot! Your brain is changing from that of a child to that of an adult and that can impact your emotions. Everything in your body and in your life is interconnected. When you are out of balance—paying too much attention to only a few parts of your life and ignoring the others, or making decisions that are not healthy—it can show up in your emotional life.

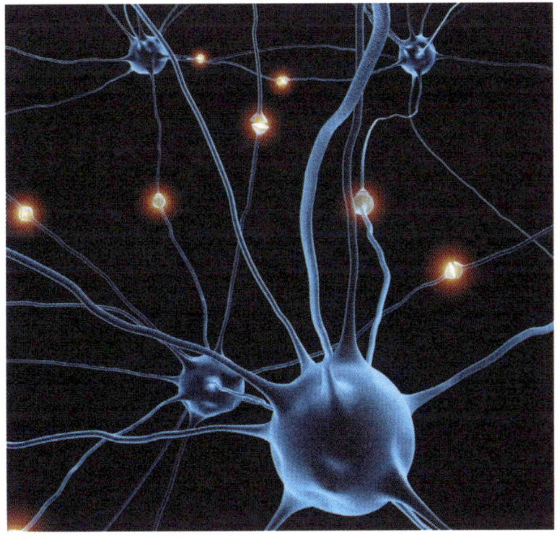

Think about your sleep, everything that you do every day, and everything you put into your body. Are you making decisions each day that are good for your brain and your emotional health?

Has your FAITH Step helped you feel better overall and helped you handle your emotions in a more positive way? Explain why or why not.

Often teenagers suffer from depression, in part because of their changing brains. If you were to feel depressed, to whom could you turn? Remember there is always help if you are feeling depressed.

SECTION THREE: **Making the Connection**

By contrast, the fruit of the Spirit is love, joy, peace, patience, kindness, generosity, faithfulness, gentleness, and self-control.

—Galatians 5:22-23

Anxiety weighs down the human heart, but a good word cheers it up.

—Proverbs 12:25

For everything there is a season . . . a time to weep, and a time to laugh; a time to mourn, and a time to dance.

—Ecclesiastes 3

One who is slow to anger is better than the mighty, and one whose temper is controlled than one who captures a city.

—Proverbs 16:32

I therefore, the prisoner in the Lord, beg you to lead a life worthy of the calling to which you have been called, with all humility and gentleness, with patience, bearing with one another in love, making every effort to maintain the unity of the Spirit in the bond of peace.

—Ephesians 4:1-3

Do not repay anyone evil for evil, but take thought for what is noble in the sight of all. If it is possible, so far as it depends on you, live peaceably with all. Beloved, never avenge yourselves, but leave room for the wrath of God; for it is written, "Vengeance is mine, I will repay, says the Lord." No, "if your enemies are hungry, feed them; if they are thirsty, give them something to drink; for by doing this you will heap burning coals on their heads." Do not be overcome by evil, but overcome evil with good.

—Romans 12:17-21

Read the verses above. Which one speaks to you? How could that verse help guide and comfort you going forward?

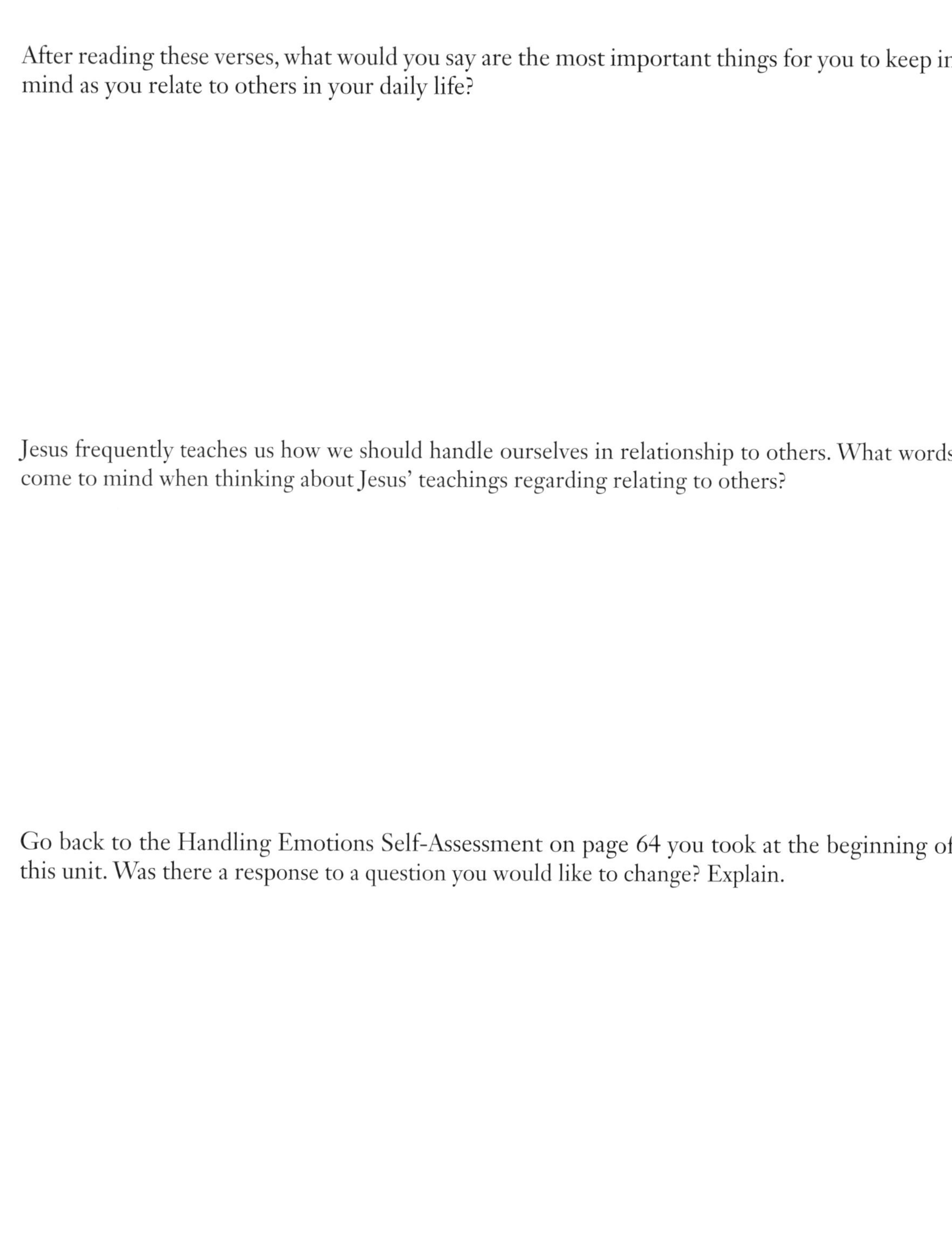

After reading these verses, what would you say are the most important things for you to keep in mind as you relate to others in your daily life?

Jesus frequently teaches us how we should handle ourselves in relationship to others. What words come to mind when thinking about Jesus' teachings regarding relating to others?

Go back to the Handling Emotions Self-Assessment on page 64 you took at the beginning of this unit. Was there a response to a question you would like to change? Explain.

In addition to your FAITH Step, what is one thing you could do differently regarding how you deal with your emotions in order to live more fully into the wisdom of these verses?

Might you need someone's help to make that change? Who might that be? How specifically could they help?

Your emotions are a great gift from God. Your emotions are meant to help you recognize situations that are healthy and unhealthy and to help guide you through those moments. It takes time to both learn to express your emotions in healthy ways, and to respectfully listen to the emotions of others. Learning what the Christian ideal is regarding how to treat others and learning how to live into your emotions and the emotions of others is an important skill. How you handle your emotions will impact everything you do going forward; your schooling, the relationships with your family and friends, and neighborhood, and your life at work.

Use the space below to reflect on this section. Remember: what you write is private, and nobody should see it unless you want to share it with them.

UNIT 6

Organization

God of Direction, guide me on the path that I am to live. You make each of us different, and my path will be different from the path that others will choose. Let me rejoice in that difference. Sometimes it does all seem useless. I have followed my path and accomplished many things I am proud of, but no matter how much I accomplish, I always want more. When I take a good, honest look at my life, I see that only one thing matters: your unconditional love. God, I want to have a positive impact on others' lives. Help me to think deeply about the ways I choose to act and to consider carefully the things I choose to believe. Let me realize that I can't accomplish everything, but I can accomplish some things. Guide me on my way so I do not stumble off your path. Today I will appreciate the differences I see around me and thank God for them. Amen.

—Brandi, age 15

SECTION ONE: **Listening to Yourself**

Do you think getting organized is boring? Many people do. Many of us think we are "too busy" to take time to get organized. Some people even make fun of people who are super organized. Let's face it; most people think there are more interesting and fun things to do besides organizing their "stuff." But people who are organized will tell you that being organized contributes to their overall well-being and is well worth the time it takes.

It can feel really good when your desk, backpack, locker, or bedroom is clean and organized. Isn't it great to be able to find what you need when you need it? When you are able to plan and organize how you want to spend your money so that some is left for savings, it's an accomplishment that feels good. When you are organized and arrive on time to school, class, work, an appointment, or get to a friend's house a little early so you are both on time, it feels good. When you know what all of your assignments are and complete them on time, you feel in control. There are benefits to being organized.

Take a few moments now to pause and listen to yourself by rating the following Self-Assessment statements about Organization. Part of who you are has to do with how you organize and use your resources of time, money, and possessions. You may discover something helpful when you examine how you organize your life through the responses you make to the statements.

Organization

The ability to keep track of and make good use of time, priorities, money, and possessions.

Rate the following 10 statements from 0–10 based on the scale below, and then write your responses on the lines provided. When you are finished, add up your responses and then shade in the total score in the **Organization** section of the Compass Self-Assessment Tool on page 3. (See pages 4 and 5 for examples.)

Never		Sometimes		Half of the Time			Most of the Time			Always
0	1	2	3	4	5	6	7	8	9	10

I feel good about the way I spend, budget, and keep track of my money. _____

I am always on time for school, work, and other commitments. _____

I organize my time and plan ahead to make sure that I allow enough time to get everything done on time. _____

I am happy with the way I organize my priorities, ensuring that I have enough time to dedicate to all the different aspects of my life. _____

I have a good method of remembering all of my assignments and other obligations. _____

My backpack, locker, and bedroom are all organized, and I can get my hands on anything I might need quickly. _____

I regularly take time to organize myself and my possessions so that I do not have to rush around at the last minute. _____

I juggle school, friends, family, and other obligations in a healthy way. _____

When thinking about how to spend my time and money, I think about others' needs as well as my own. _____

Most days I accomplish all of the things I set out to do that day. _____

TOTAL _____

Looking carefully at the scores you gave yourself, do you see one area that could use more attention, one area that if you paid more attention to it would benefit or improve your life? Think concretely as you create a FAITH Step for yourself that you feel willing to commit to over the next several weeks. This is only for you, so make sure it is something that you really feel is important to you and fits who you are. Write your FAITH Step on the next page, and then share aloud with at least one person. List one step that is: Focused, Action Oriented, Inspired, Time Sensitive, and Heartfelt and Honest. (See pages 6 and 7 for instructions and a sample FAITH Step.)

Create a FAITH Step

Area of Wellness: Organization

Date: ______

Overarching Goal:	
Focused: **A**ction: **I**nspired: **T**ime Sensitive: **H**eartfelt and Honest:	
Obstacles:	Solutions:
Final FAITH Step:	

SECTION TWO: **Learning**

Perhaps you know people who are disorganized. Friends who never seems to know where anything is, don't know how much money they have, who have trouble keeping track of due dates for homework, or even knowing what their assignments are.

It may be that they are always late, and that their room, car, or locker is a mess. If you lend them something, you don't get it back because they have lost it—you get the idea. They are often very good people in all other respects. They might drop what they are doing if someone needs help, they are generous, they are thoughtful, and they are fun, but they struggle with keeping their "things together."

Disorganized people might get "stressed out" more than others due to their disorganization. They might get stressed out when they realize a big research paper that they had forgotten all about is due tomorrow, or when they can't find a friend's jacket they borrowed. It can also be that they are already stressed and that leads to their disorganization. It can go both ways.

Disorganization can cause a stress cycle. Disorganization often leads to stress (the assignment not completed on time, the jacket lost), which causes the person to focus on other things (frantically writing the paper, looking for the jacket or struggling to find the money to replace it). This means the person isn't able to think about how they could be better organized, which causes more stress. It can keep going and going in a seemingly endless cycle.

Disorganization also can lead to a feeling of being off balance. This can then affect other areas of life: grades suffer when someone is disorganized, relationships can suffer when someone is always late, and employers don't often keep disorganized workers on their payroll for long. There are some areas in life in which we have less control over organization, but that doesn't mean we have to settle for being disorganized in other areas of our lives. If any of this sounds familiar, know that you don't have to get stuck in the cycle of stress caused by disorganization. By making choices about what you focus on, and choosing to spend a few minutes a day on organization, you can move from the stress of disorganization to experiencing a feeling of being energized and empowered simply by being organized.

Getting organized is a lot like exercising. If we do it occasionally, we won't see much change to our physical well-being. When we exercise on a regular basis over a period of time, however, we become stronger, faster, more fit, and more energetic. In other words, we experience all the benefits of exercising when we exercise regularly. The same thing is true with organization. To experience the benefits, you need to set aside time to get organized on an ongoing basis. If you are a person who could improve in the area of organization, remember that small steps taken on a daily basis can make a big difference.

Becoming organized in any area of your life—such as caring for your possessions, handling money, keeping your bedroom, your calendar, or several of these areas at the same time—means you need to form new habits. This can be challenging. It is not what you are used to, and therefore it isn't your "normal." It will feel uncomfortable, time-consuming, and maybe even draining at first. That feeling won't last. The longer you stick to your new habits, the more "comfortable" they will become. That's how it works when you are making a new "normal" for yourself.

People who study this kind of thing say it takes at least twenty-one days to form a new habit, whether it is a good or bad habit. As you explore making a new habit in your life, be aware it will take at least three weeks, so if you have feelings of discomfort, if you fail once or twice, keep trying, don't give up. Change takes time, but it is a good use of time.

To Form a New Habit:

- **Know what habit you are trying to form, and focus on just that one habit for a while.** It can be as simple as putting dates on the calendar, keeping up with assignments by putting them into your phone calendar with alerts, picking up your room every night before bed, cleaning out your locker or backpack and then reorganizing it once a month, or creating a budget for yourself. It can be anything that helps you feel more organized and in control.
- **Think of one or two steps to move toward your new habit of being organized.** You might try recording appointments and assignments on your phone, buying a planner, or getting bags to collect what you no longer need in your room.
- **Set dates and timelines for getting things done.**
- **Do what you need to do repeatedly until it becomes your new habit.**
- **Ask someone to help you get started and to support you as you grow this new skill.**

Living It

Remember that "being organized" refers to organization of priorities, time, money, and stuff. People who are organized will tell you that being organized can give you space to breathe.

How do you understand the statement that being organized can give you space to breathe? Does it make sense to you? Explain.

The way we manage our time reveals a lot about our priorities. Does the way you are currently prioritizing things line up with what you say you value? How could you change that?

Where do you feel the most organized in your life? Time? Priorities? Possessions? Money? How does that make you feel? How does that affect you?

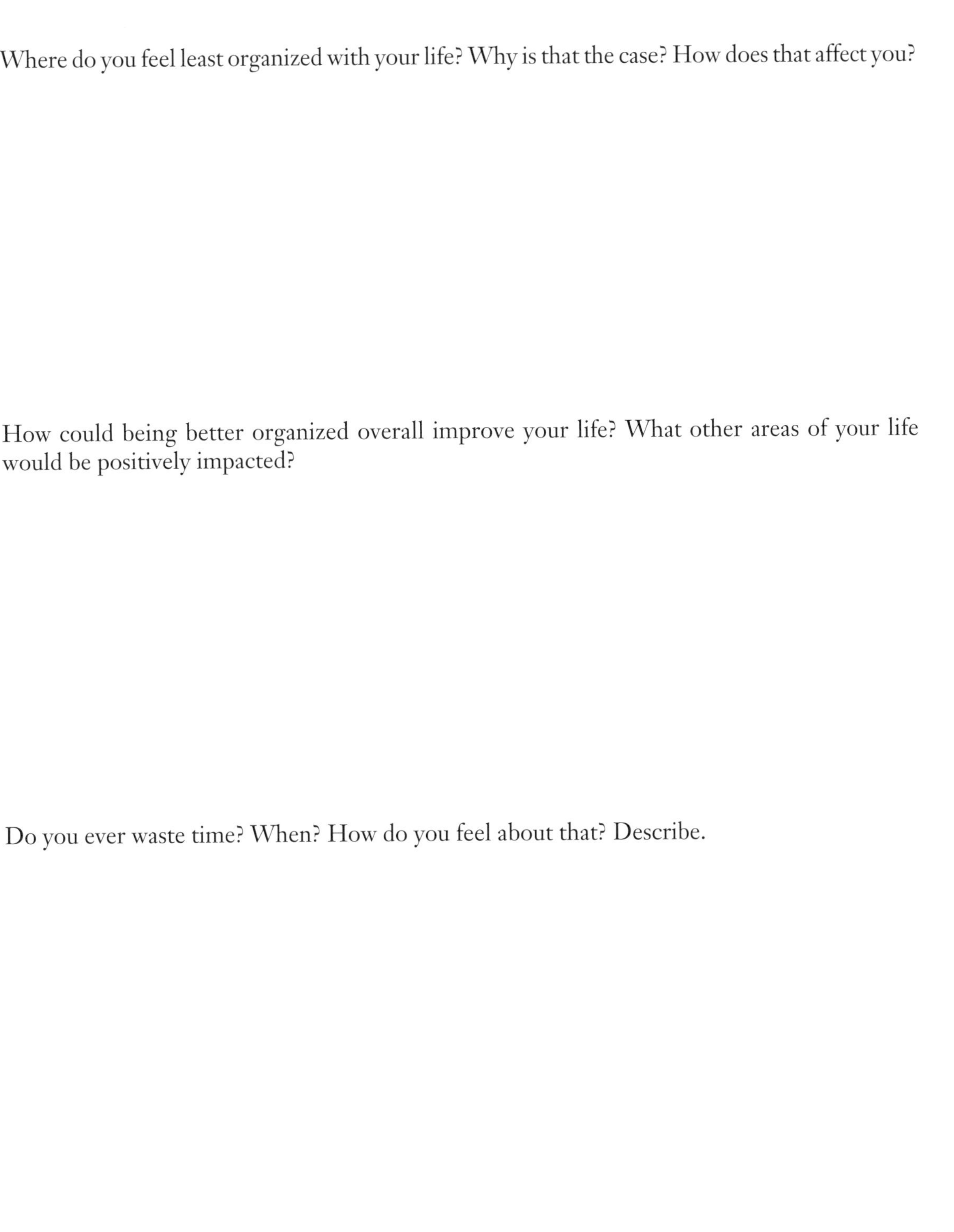

Where do you feel least organized with your life? Why is that the case? How does that affect you?

How could being better organized overall improve your life? What other areas of your life would be positively impacted?

Do you ever waste time? When? How do you feel about that? Describe.

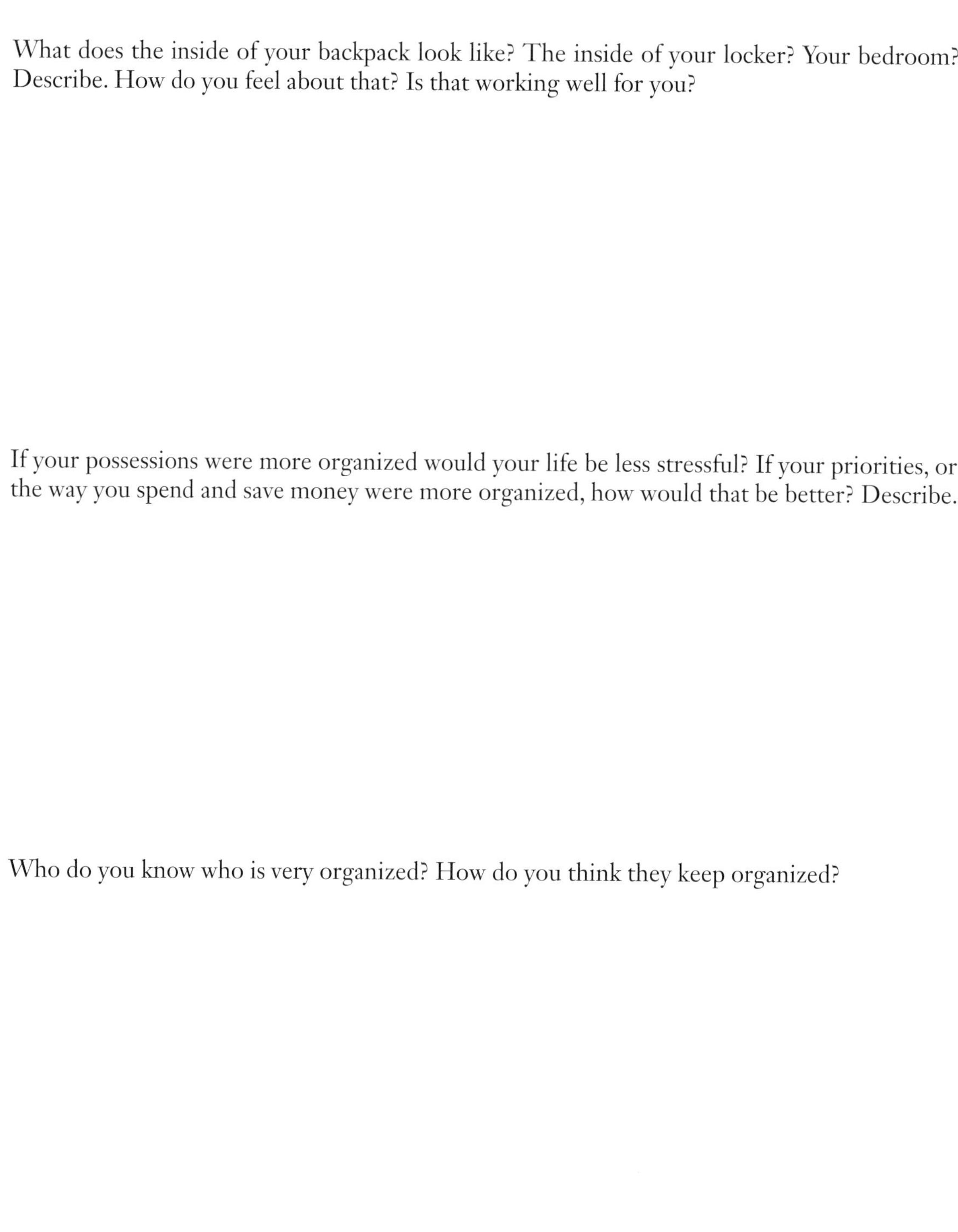

What does the inside of your backpack look like? The inside of your locker? Your bedroom? Describe. How do you feel about that? Is that working well for you?

If your possessions were more organized would your life be less stressful? If your priorities, or the way you spend and save money were more organized, how would that be better? Describe.

Who do you know who is very organized? How do you think they keep organized?

What could you learn from them that might help you get better organized?

You'll hear people talk about "stewardship" on occasion at church. While it generally refers to giving to the church in some way (for example, giving time, talent, or money), thinking about stewardship can also be an opportunity to examine how people organize and take care of the things in their lives.

What if, before you died, someone asked you to take a look at how you had been a steward of your life? What if you had to explain how you had spent your time and energy, where you spent your money, how you used what you had received?

This would be an exercise in examining how you had practiced being a good steward of the good things you had been given over your lifetime: time, energy, material things, relationships, the earth, opportunities, and the multitude of other things that God had given you.

What do you think about the idea that God cares about how we spend or organize our time, our money, and the gifts and talents we have? That we have been given them to help bring God's love to the world?

A place for everything, everything in its place.
—Benjamin Franklin

SECTION THREE: **Making the Connection**

But all things should be done decently and in order.

—1 Corinthians 14:40

For everything there is a season, and a time for every matter under heaven.

—Ecclesiastes 3:1

For which of you, intending to build a tower, does not first sit down and estimate the cost, to see whether he has enough to complete it?

—Luke 14:28

He looked up and saw rich people putting their gifts into the treasury; he also saw a poor widow put in two small copper coins. He said, "Truly I tell you, this poor widow has put in more than all of them; for all of them have contributed out of their abundance, but she out of her poverty has put in all she had to live on."

—Luke 21:1-4

Do not store up for yourselves treasures on earth, where moth and rust consume and where thieves break in and steal; but store up for yourselves treasures in heaven, where neither moth nor rust consumes and where thieves do not break in and steal. For where your treasure is, there your heart will be also.

—Matthew 6:19-21

Read through the verses above. What values do you see expressed here related to organization, money, and possessions?

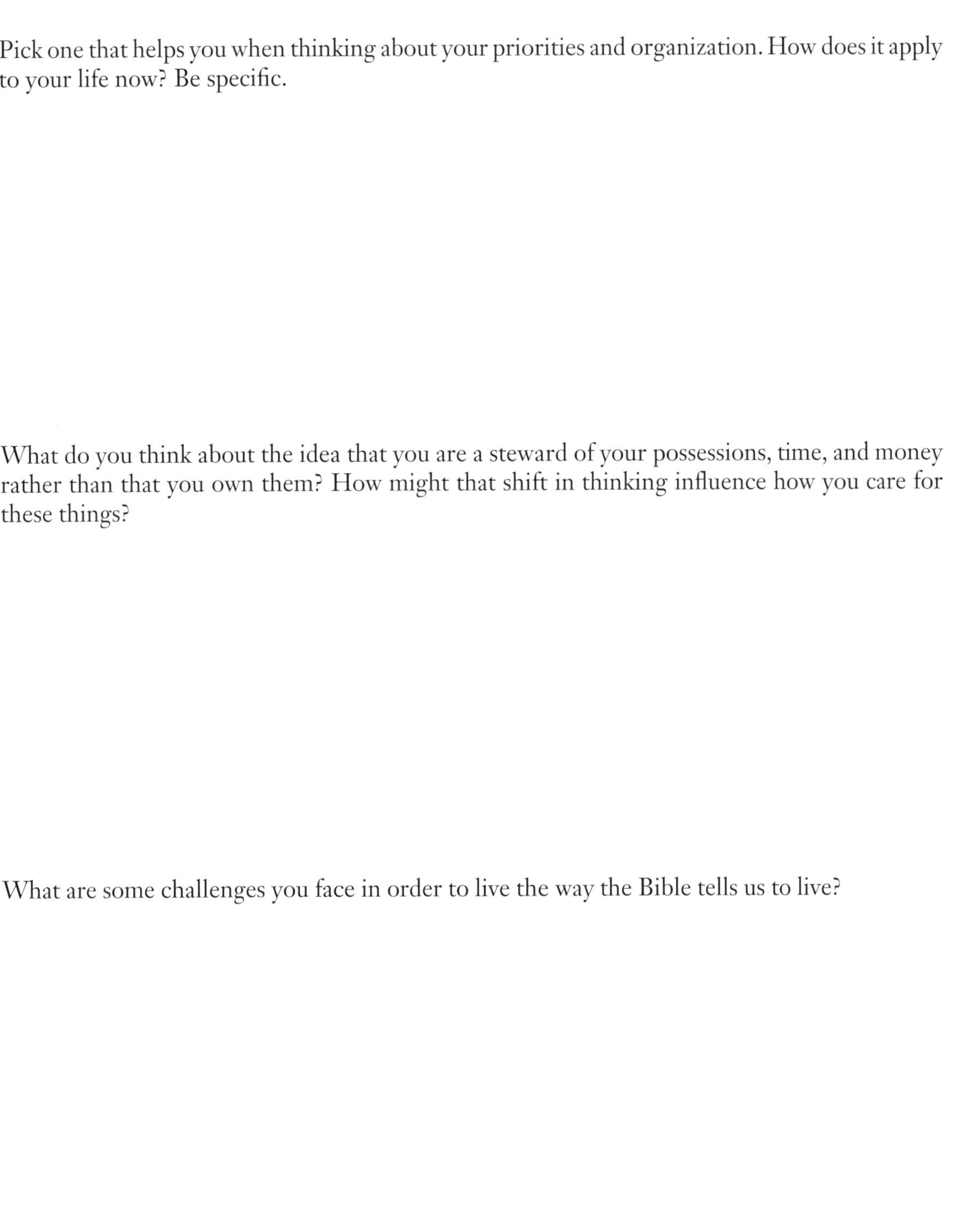

Pick one that helps you when thinking about your priorities and organization. How does it apply to your life now? Be specific.

What do you think about the idea that you are a steward of your possessions, time, and money rather than that you own them? How might that shift in thinking influence how you care for these things?

What are some challenges you face in order to live the way the Bible tells us to live?

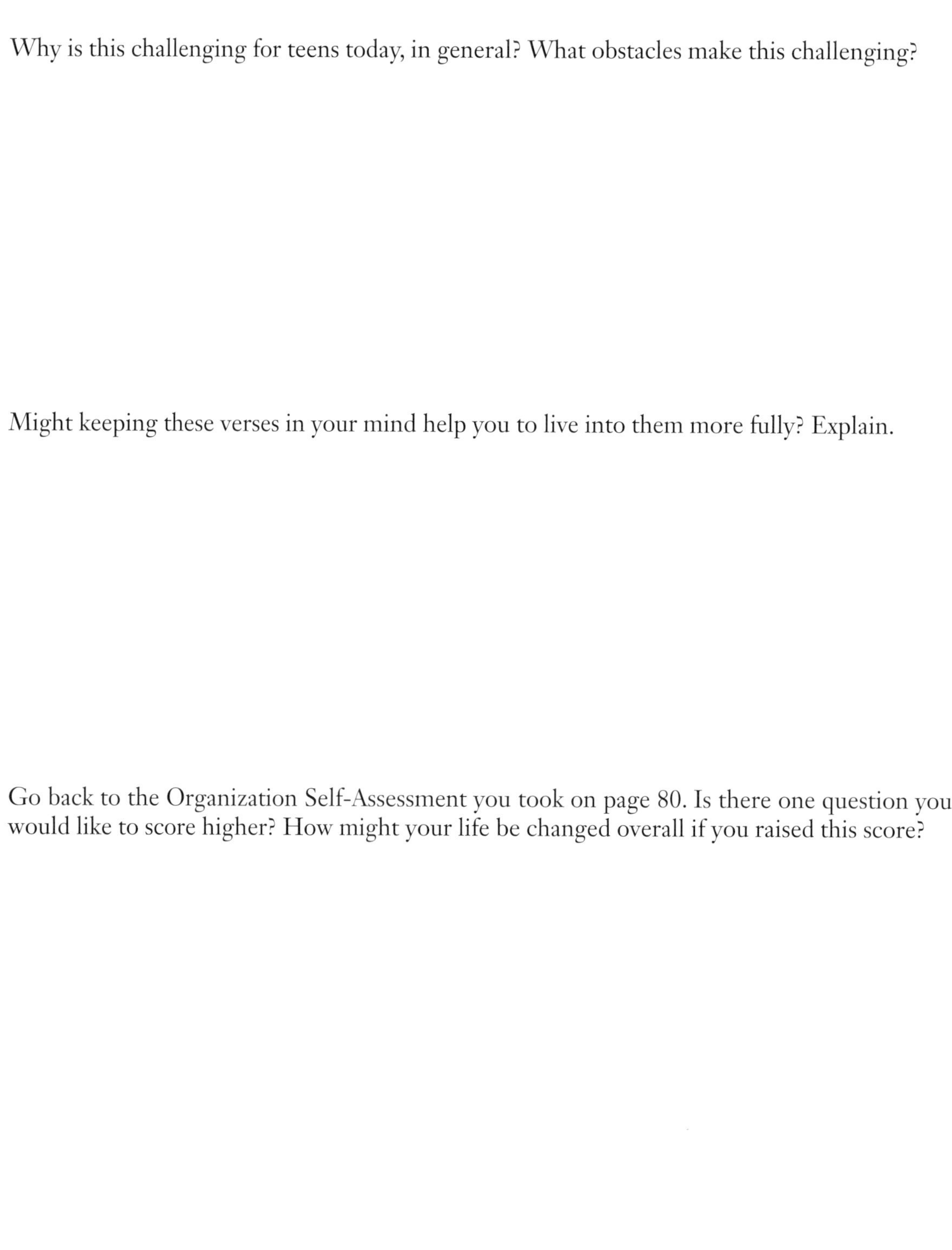

Why is this challenging for teens today, in general? What obstacles make this challenging?

Might keeping these verses in your mind help you to live into them more fully? Explain.

Go back to the Organization Self-Assessment you took on page 80. Is there one question you would like to score higher? How might your life be changed overall if you raised this score?

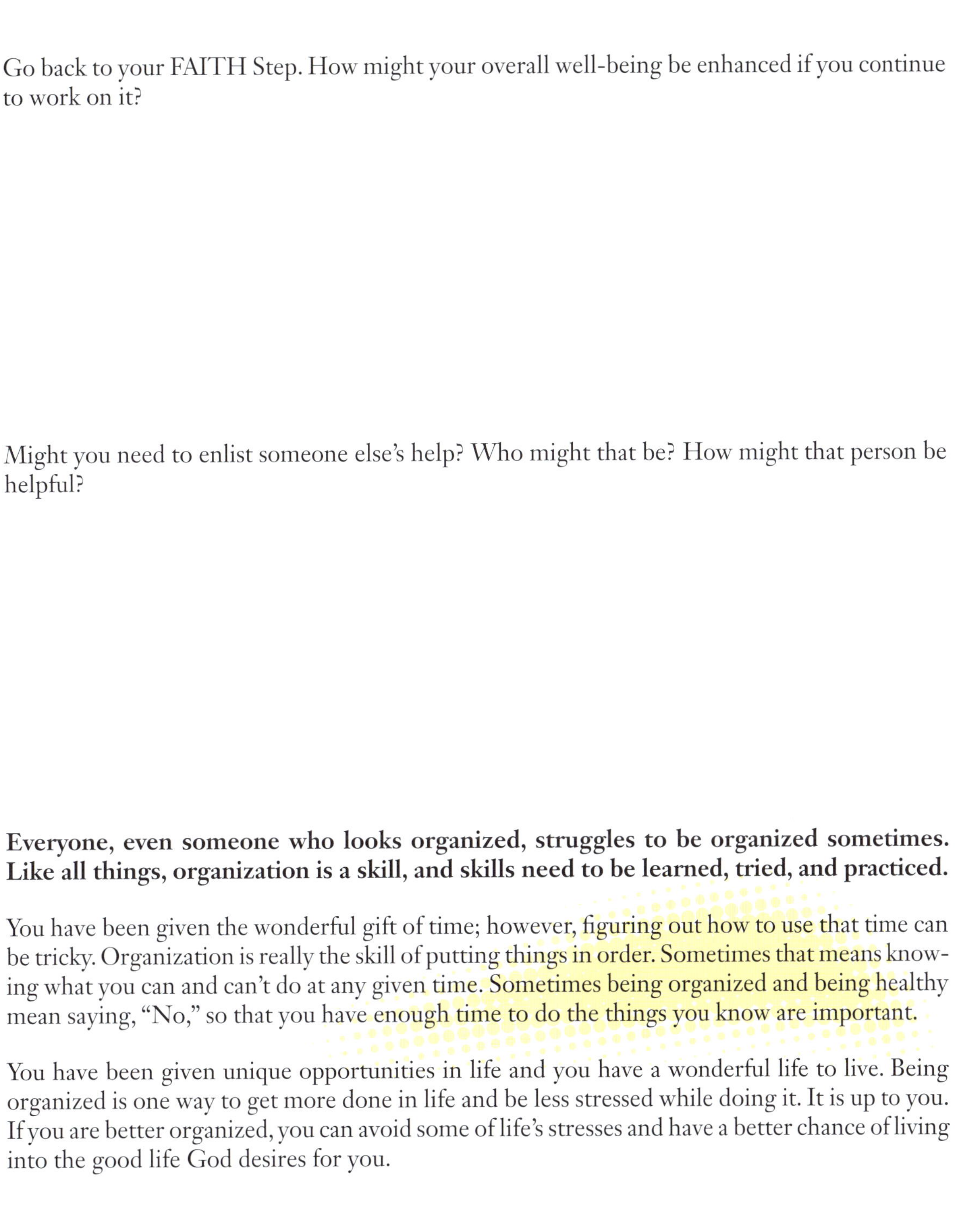

Go back to your FAITH Step. How might your overall well-being be enhanced if you continue to work on it?

Might you need to enlist someone else's help? Who might that be? How might that person be helpful?

Everyone, even someone who looks organized, struggles to be organized sometimes. Like all things, organization is a skill, and skills need to be learned, tried, and practiced.

You have been given the wonderful gift of time; however, figuring out how to use that time can be tricky. Organization is really the skill of putting things in order. Sometimes that means knowing what you can and can't do at any given time. Sometimes being organized and being healthy mean saying, "No," so that you have enough time to do the things you know are important.

You have been given unique opportunities in life and you have a wonderful life to live. Being organized is one way to get more done in life and be less stressed while doing it. It is up to you. If you are better organized, you can avoid some of life's stresses and have a better chance of living into the good life God desires for you.

Use the space below to reflect on this section. Remember: what you write is private, and nobody should see it unless you want to share it with them.

UNIT 7

School and Work

Lord of all Wisdom, you give us minds and hearts to know and love your creation. Make me eager to learn, patient with my mistakes and failures, and quick to forgive others who have been unfair to me, so that I can use my knowledge to build a better world. Amen.

—Gregory, age 18

SECTION ONE: Listening to Yourself

Whether you love it, hate it, or are indifferent to it, school is one of the most important parts of your life. Some say going to school is like your job; it is what you have to do and where you need to do your best. Why? So you can go to college? So you can get a job? So you can be a well-educated citizen?

Maybe there is another reason. There is a story about a student who asked her wise teacher, "I want to make a difference in the world. What does the world need me to do?" The teacher responded: "Do what makes you feel most alive, because the world needs more people who are fully alive." **Maybe the reason you go to school is to help you find and begin to explore what makes you feel fully alive, how to best use your God-given talents, and to equip yourself to live into that passion and those talents. And maybe it is meant to help prepare you so that you can help make the world a better place.** Maybe you have already thought about school this way. Maybe this is a new idea. Why do you think it's important for you to go to school?

We invite you to take the School/Work Self-Assessment to see how you are engaging school and, if you have one, your job. Take a few moments now to listen to yourself by rating the following ten statements in the assessment. This is intended to be a tool for you to pay attention to how *you* think things are going for you, rather than what your teachers, parents or guardians, or friends are saying. This is just for you.

School and Work

The ability to get the most out of educational, volunteer, and employment opportunities.

Rate the following 10 statements from 0–10 based on the scale below, and then write your responses on the lines provided. When you are finished, add up your responses and then shade in the total score in the **School and Work** section of the Compass Self-Assessment Tool on page 3. (See pages 4 and 5 for examples.)

Never		Sometimes		Half of the Time			Most of the Time			Always
0	1	2	3	4	5	6	7	8	9	10

I feel good about my overall involvement in school, knowing I'm doing my best. _____

I am personally satisfied with my grades. _____

I am satisfied with the way I participate in my classes, extracurricular activities, volunteer work, or job. _____

I am pleased with the connections I have with the teachers and staff at school. _____

I feel good about the relationships I have with other students and how those relationships impact my all-around success at school. _____

I am confident that my school/volunteer/sports/job performance is helping to guide my future in a positive way. _____

I am confident that the effort I put into my school/job will serve me well in the future. _____

I feel good about the way my decisions regarding alcohol and other drugs impact my learning, volunteer, and/or job performance. _____

I am comfortable with the way my employment and other outside activities affect my school and family life. _____

I am using my God-given talents and passions at school, work, or in the community. _____

TOTAL _____

Looking carefully at the scores you gave yourself, do you see one area that could use more attention, one area that if you paid more attention to it would benefit or improve your life? Think concretely as you create a FAITH Step for yourself that you feel willing to commit to over the next several weeks. This is only for you, so make sure it is something that you really feel is important to you and fits who you are. Write your FAITH Step on the next page, and then share aloud with at least one person. List one step that is: Focused, Action Oriented, Inspired, Time Sensitive, and Heartfelt and Honest. (See pages 6 and 7 for instructions and a sample FAITH Step.)

Create a FAITH Step

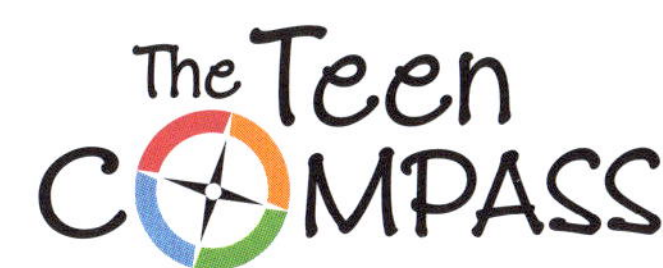

Area of Wellness: School and Work

Date: ____________

Overarching Goal:	
Focused: **A**ction: **I**nspired: **T**ime Sensitive: **H**eartfelt and Honest:	
Obstacles:	Solutions:
Final FAITH Step:	

SECTION TWO: **Learning**

At this point of your life, you have to go to school and school is a huge part of your life. Many parts of your life are being formed at school: your work ethic, your ability to interact with all kinds of people, your sense of responsibility, time management, and organizational skills, to name a few. And this doesn't even include what you are learning in the classroom.

What are some words you would use to describe your school experience? Write them in the space below. Write anything that comes to mind—this is your notebook. You get to pick the words; so choose the words you feel truly reflect how you feel about school, both positive and negative.

Did you use the word "fun" anywhere? School can be fun, and there are many times when learning can be a truly pleasurable experience. School can be thought provoking: it can open your mind to new ideas and new concepts. School can also be frustrating, it can be confusing, it can be stressful, and it can be exhausting.

Believe it or not, your school experience depends just as much on you as it does on your teachers. Your attitude toward school and how you participate in school can determine how much you will get out of it. For example, if you believe that school is some sort of prison that keeps you from doing what you want to do all day, and you spend your time watching the clock hoping for the end of the school day, then you probably won't get much out of it. On the other hand, if you believe school is a great opportunity, a privilege, and has something wonderful to offer you, then you are likely to engage it in a positive way. It's all in how you look at it.

Your overall health can influence how you view school and how well you do there. If things are difficult at home, then school might become an escape, or it might be difficult for you to pay attention. If your physical health is poor, if you are dealing with constant pain or some other condition, it most likely will make learning difficult and keeping up with school activities a challenge. If you are feeling depressed, school can be difficult, too.

The way you choose to participate at school also affects your overall health and wellness in other areas—all areas of your life and all areas of your wellness are interconnected. So how you choose to participate in school is very important. If you choose to see the commitments of work and school as a source of opportunity and growth, which will help prepare you for the future, they have the potential to have an overall positive effect on your life.

Bob Dylan received the Medal of Freedom from the President of the United States in 2012. Bob Dylan is a singer and songwriter who has made lasting contributions to folk and rock music from the 1960s to today. Millions of people love to listen to his words and music, and as the President said that day, "There is not a bigger giant in the history of American music."

What many people don't know is that Bob has a son, Jakob Dylan, who is an aspiring musician. It is not easy to be successful in the world of music; musicians like Bob Dylan have had to work incredibly hard for many years just to get a record deal. Jakob has an even bigger challenge: being compared to his father. People are always saying to him, "You certainly have big shoes to fill." Most folks who hear this statement don't like it and Jakob probably doesn't like it, either. While it could mean he has a lot of work to do, it could also mean he is not as good as his father. Hearing comments like that can be discouraging.

Jakob Dylan will never be his father nor should he try to be. He must live his own uniquely special life. The same is true for you. The only shoes you have to fill are yours. Nobody else's. No one can. You get to live your own life.

You were given a lot when you were given the gift of life. You were given a unique body and a unique spirit. You were given the capacity to feel a huge range of emotions. You were given relationships to nurture and enjoy.

You were given a marvelous mind capable of learning, understanding, questioning, and seeing things that no one else can see. You were also given skills and talents, along with a unique personality that is just yours. **When you combine all the different things you have been given, you see that you have been given the fantastic opportunity to become this unique person who can do what only you can do! What a gift that is!**

The thing is, you don't just instantly become this person. You grow into who you are over years and years. Your experiences, your values, your relationships, and your faith shape and form you, not just into whom you want to be, but also into whom God made you to be and whom God dreams you to be. Your school and your job are places where you are given opportunities to find out how you are unique, what you can and can't do, and what you love to do. They help you grow into who you truly are. Other places that might also do this for you are your church, your home, service organizations, sports, clubs, or camps. These all are places that can be formative as well as providing opportunities for making friends and having great fun.

Your job is to figure out who YOU are, so you can continue growing into who you are meant to be. Your job is to find out how your unique gifts intersect with the world's needs. It is tremendous work, the most meaningful work you can do. It might be frightening or overwhelming or empowering when you think about it. Something important to remember: you aren't in it alone. There are many people who can help you: friends, teachers, coaches, leaders at church, parents, or grandparents. You can probably think of several others who can help you figure out who you are. The world is what you make of it, which is what is so exciting!

Living It

Do you have a positive attitude in school? Will your attitude help you develop a positive future? Remember that you can change your attitude if it is not serving you well.

What is school like for you right now? Explain why that is.

Is your involvement in sports and other extracurricular activities meaningful for you? Explain.

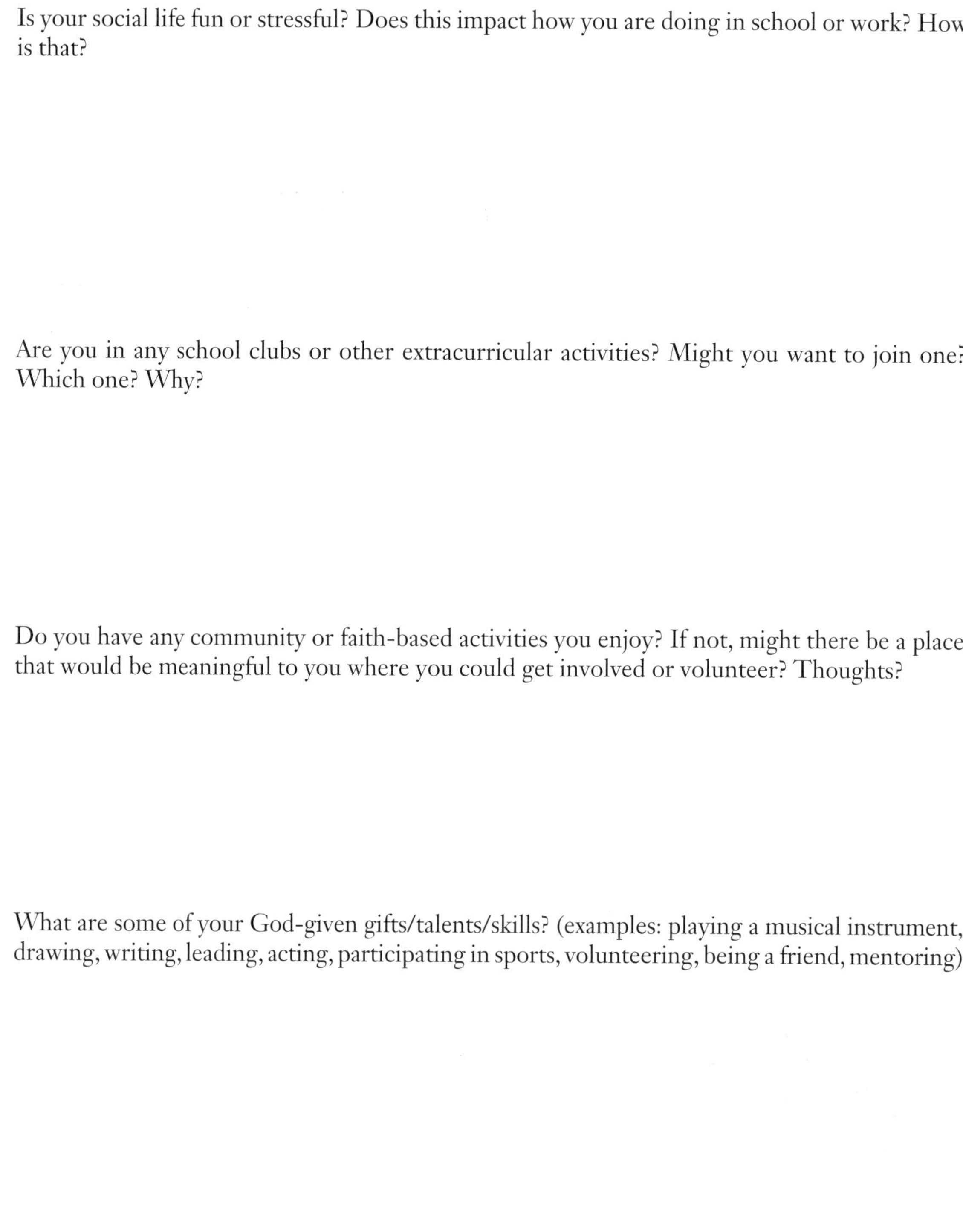

Is your social life fun or stressful? Does this impact how you are doing in school or work? How is that?

Are you in any school clubs or other extracurricular activities? Might you want to join one? Which one? Why?

Do you have any community or faith-based activities you enjoy? If not, might there be a place that would be meaningful to you where you could get involved or volunteer? Thoughts?

What are some of your God-given gifts/talents/skills? (examples: playing a musical instrument, drawing, writing, leading, acting, participating in sports, volunteering, being a friend, mentoring)

How could you make your gifts or talents more available to others?

Do you feel that the adults in your life recognize your unique talents? How could you make people more aware of your abilities?

Do you use some of those talents at school? If not, could you? Where and how?

What are some words that describe who you are now? A student? An athlete? An employee? A friend? A volunteer? School gives you many opportunities to be many different things. Are you comfortable with the roles you are playing at school now? Would you like to try something new? Explain.

Who you are in the future will be impacted by who you are today. What are some words that you would like to use to describe yourself in the future? Are you heading in the right direction?

How can school or a job help you grow into the words you want to be able to use when describing yourself in the future? What part do you need to play in making that happen?

Out of all the things that you do, what is most important to you? Your response might be a clue about what is unique about you and how you can give back to the world.

When you think that God has a dream for you, what do you think it might be? What makes you think so?

What are some ways you can listen for what God dreams for you and begin to live into that dream?

Think back to your FAITH Step. What is one small thing you can do starting today that could help you engage school and work more fully?

SECTION THREE: **Making the Connection**

All these are activated by one and the same Spirit, who allots to each one individually just as the Spirit chooses.

—1 Corinthians 12:11

Whatever your task, put yourselves into it, as done for the Lord and not for your masters.

—Colossians 3:23

For surely I know the plans I have for you, says the Lord, plans for your welfare and not for harm, to give you a future with hope.

—Jeremiah 29:11

Do not work for the food that perishes, but for the food that endures for eternal life, which the Son of Man will give you. For it is on him that God the Father has set his seal.

—John 6:27

From whom the whole body, joined and knit together by every ligament with which it is equipped, as each part is working properly, promotes the body's growth in building itself up in love.

—Ephesians 4:16

And there are varieties of activities, but it is the same God who activates all of them in everyone.

—1 Corinthians 12:6

Look at the verses above. How can they help guide you as you think about how to best engage in your work at school and elsewhere?

Modern teens are under a lot of pressure to perform well—for many reasons. Do any of these verses give you a different perspective on grades and performance? What are they saying to you?

Why is it hard for teens in your world to live by these words?

What message are you getting from the scripture about work and your future?

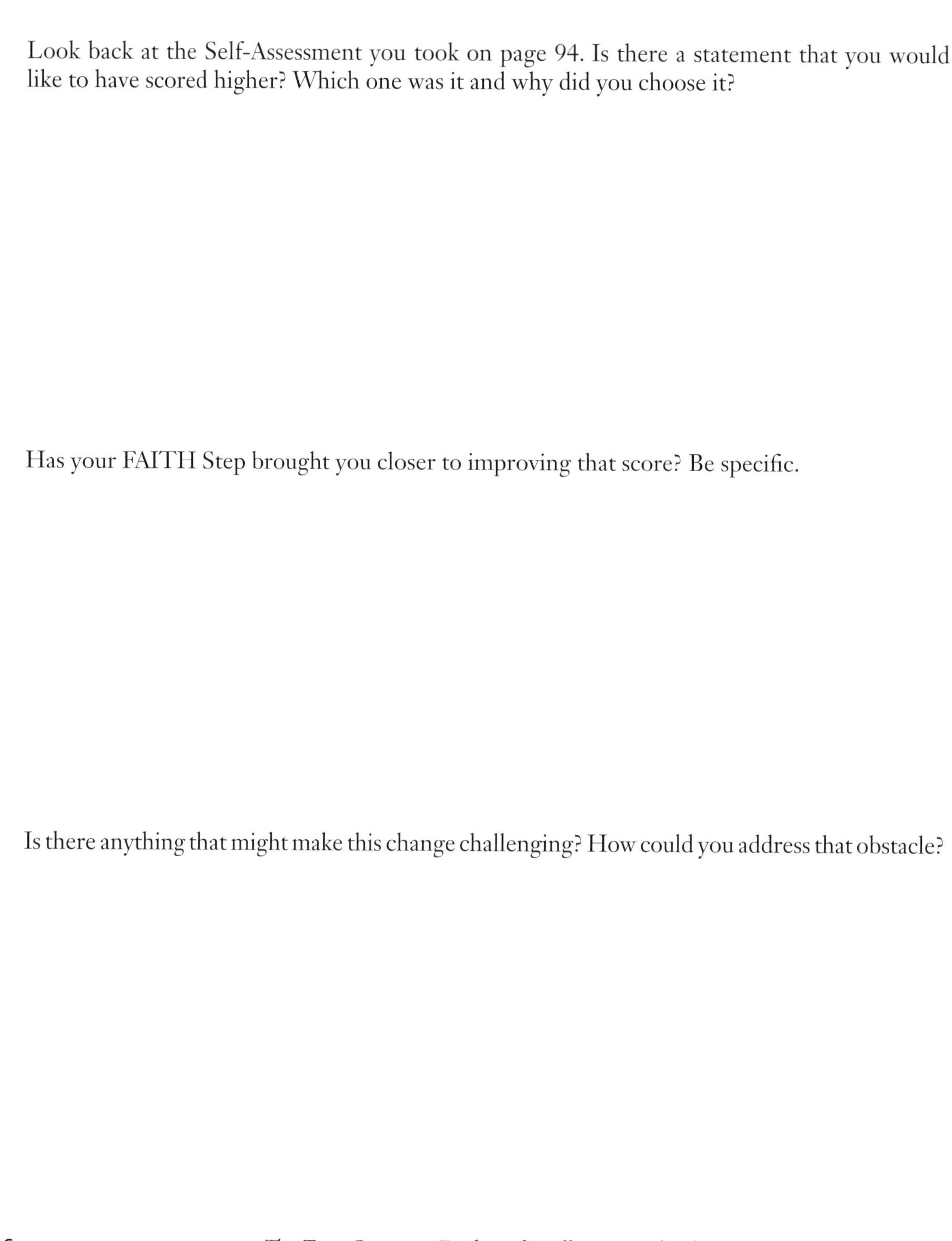

Look back at the Self-Assessment you took on page 94. Is there a statement that you would like to have scored higher? Which one was it and why did you choose it?

Has your FAITH Step brought you closer to improving that score? Be specific.

Is there anything that might make this change challenging? How could you address that obstacle?

Do you need help from anyone to make this happen? Who would that be, and how could they help? Be specific.

You are living and learning about life every day, both at school and outside of school. What you learn will help you become who you are and who you are meant to be. It is up to you to take advantage of the opportunities around you. These years are important. Enjoy and learn as much as you can, and enjoy the world God has created for you.

Use the space below to reflect on this section. Remember: what you write is private, and nobody should see it unless you want to share it with them.

Unit 8

Care for the Body

Dear God, Thank you for my body, for it holds my life together. May I live my life well inside it so I may live long in this world and forever in heaven. Amen.

—*The Lion Book of 1000 Prayers*, p. 152

SECTION ONE: Listening to Yourself

In our 21st-century culture, there is much emphasis placed on how our bodies look. We are told subtly that it is more important to look a certain way, to be a certain weight, and to wear certain kinds of clothes, than it is to be healthy. **Caring for our bodies and how we present them is a lot more complicated and important than having the latest hairstyle or wearing those hot shoes.** Our bodies are important. They were given to us by God and now it is our responsibility to care for them.

Take a few moments to complete the following Care for the Body Self-Assessment. Remember, no one else is going to read this unless you ask him or her to—it is intended to be private. This is an opportunity for you to pause and take a look at where you are right now in terms of caring for your body. Answer each question honestly.

Care for the Body

The ability to build healthy habits and practices around your physical well-being and to end unhealthy habits.

Rate the following 10 statements from 0–10 based on the scale below, and then write your responses on the lines provided. When you are finished, add up your responses and then shade in the total score in the **Care for the Body** section of the Compass Self-Assessment Tool on page 3. (See pages 4 and 5 for examples.)

Never		Sometimes		Half of the Time			Most of the Time			Always
0	1	2	3	4	5	6	7	8	9	10

The daily choices I make about what I eat and drink are healthy. _____

I feel good about the amount of regular exercise I get. _____

I determine what is healthy and right for me, in terms of weight and appearance, rather letting my peers or the culture determine that for me. _____

I go to the doctor and dentist for regular checkups and talk to someone about a health problem as soon as it arises. _____

I am comfortable with my sexuality and know that my sexual decisions are healthy and safe for me, physically, emotionally, and spiritually. _____

I Corinthians 6:19 says, "Your body is a temple of the Holy Spirit." I treat my body accordingly by the respect I show it. _____

My current weight is healthy for me. _____

I feel confident that my decisions regarding drugs, alcohol, and tobacco are serving me well. _____

Most days I get at least eight hours of sleep during normal sleeping hours. _____

I have positive feelings about my relationship with food (what I eat, why I eat, and how often I eat). _____

TOTAL _____

Looking carefully at the scores you gave yourself, do you see one area that could use more attention, one area that if you paid more attention to it would benefit or improve your life? Think concretely as you create a FAITH Step for yourself that you feel willing to commit to over the next several weeks. This is only for you, so make sure it is something that you really feel is important to you and fits who you are. Write your FAITH Step on the next page, and then share aloud with at least one person. List one step that is: Focused, Action Oriented, Inspired, Time Sensitive, and Heartfelt and Honest. (See pages 6 and 7 for instructions and a sample FAITH Step.)

Create a FAITH Step

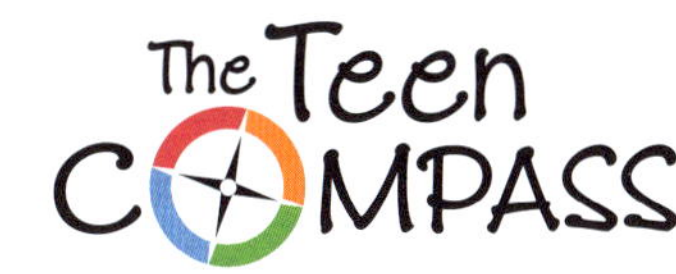

Area of Wellness: Care for the Body

Date: ______

Overarching Goal:

Focused:

Action:

Inspired:

Time Sensitive:

Heartfelt and Honest:

Obstacles:	Solutions:

Final FAITH Step:

SECTION TWO: **Learning**

Who wouldn't want a new car? They are very exciting to own. New cars look great, feel great, smell great, and run smoothly. Wouldn't it be great if new cars always looked, sounded, felt, and ran the same as the day we got them? But they don't. Cars get scratches and dents. Engines lose a bit of pickup over the years. And that "new-car smell" doesn't last forever.

In order for our cars to do what we want them to do, we have to care for them. We have to wash them, repair them when they are broken, fill their tanks with gas, change the oil and filters, and rotate the tires. Even with all that maintenance, the average car usually only lasts around ten years. If we are fortunate and vigilant with care, maybe we can help our car last a few years longer. The human body, on the other hand, is expected to live about eighty years—much longer than a car. If we think it is important to care for our cars to keep them running well, think how much more important it is, then, to give our bodies intentional care on a regular basis. Our life is the greatest gift we will ever receive.

God has given us life and has given us everything we need to live a good life. Your body is an incredible gift. It is a unique combination of the genes that come from your family's genetic histories. This, along with the medical care you access, influences your physical health. The simple, day-to-day choices you make regarding your body is another very important factor that contributes to how you feel and how you look and how healthy you are.

Just as you would put good quality gasoline into your car and work to maintain the car as best you can, you need to care for and refuel your body, as well. This is so your body can take you where you need to go, and on whatever adventures you want to experience, much like your car does. **What you put into your body makes a big difference.**

You are now at a place in your life where you have more choices over what you will and will not eat than you did when you were younger. Good fuel means good performance. You get to choose what to eat and how often. Eating a balanced diet not only makes you perform better at sports or in school, but also makes you feel better.

If you run a car continually without stopping, eventually the engine will overheat or seize up and finally stop working completely. Your body also needs rest. **When you sleep, many things are going on in every part of your body: your brain is processing the information it gathered during the day, your muscles are relaxing and growing, new cells are being created, and any injuries you have are healing.** When you get enough sleep, you have more energy, you learn better, you tend to feel better, and you can handle stress better.

Sometimes when we get are tired, yet need to get something done, it is tempting to use something artificial to get that energy, like caffeine for example. Any artificial stimulant, if abused, can hurt instead of heal. Sometimes it might even be tempting to turn to alcohol or other drugs to feel a little better, as well. This can be very dangerous.

When one part of your life is out of balance, you may feel the effects in your body or in other parts of your life. If you aren't getting enough sleep, your immune system can weaken, making you more susceptible to getting sick. If you are an athlete and start making poor choices about what you eat, your performance might suffer. You also may be cranky, which may impact important relationships in your life.

What is your body telling you? You have been given a tremendous gift by God! It is a gift that will go everywhere you go, every day for the rest of your life. Remember, you can't live your life without this body of yours, so caring for it is important.

Living It

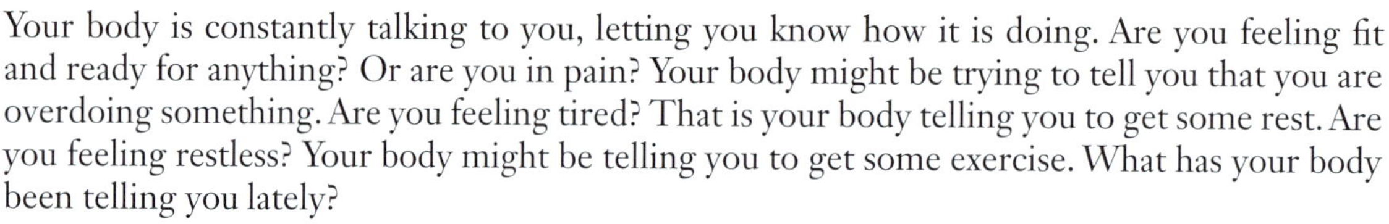

Your body is constantly talking to you, letting you know how it is doing. Are you feeling fit and ready for anything? Or are you in pain? Your body might be trying to tell you that you are overdoing something. Are you feeling tired? That is your body telling you to get some rest. Are you feeling restless? Your body might be telling you to get some exercise. What has your body been telling you lately?

Imagine that your body could write you a letter telling you how you are doing right now, where it needs care, or what it would like you to do to feel better. What might it say?

Are there things you are doing right now or might be thinking about doing that will have long-term effects on your body, such as using alcohol or other drugs, harming yourself, smoking, or being sexually active? How might doing these things impact your health?

How people care for their bodies can be an indicator of how they feel about themselves. What does the way you care for your body say about how you feel about yourself? Consider such things as eating, sleeping, sex, and exercise.

What about your body do you appreciate the most? What important things does it allow you to do?

How can you show your body that you appreciate the gift that it is? Getting more sleep? Getting more exercise? Eating better food? Being safe sexually? Other ideas?

How do you show respect to your body? How does that make you feel all over? Think mind, body, and soul.

Is there anyway in which you do not respect your body, such as smoking, using alcohol and other drugs, cutting, or eating junk food? How does that make you feel? Think mind, body, and soul.

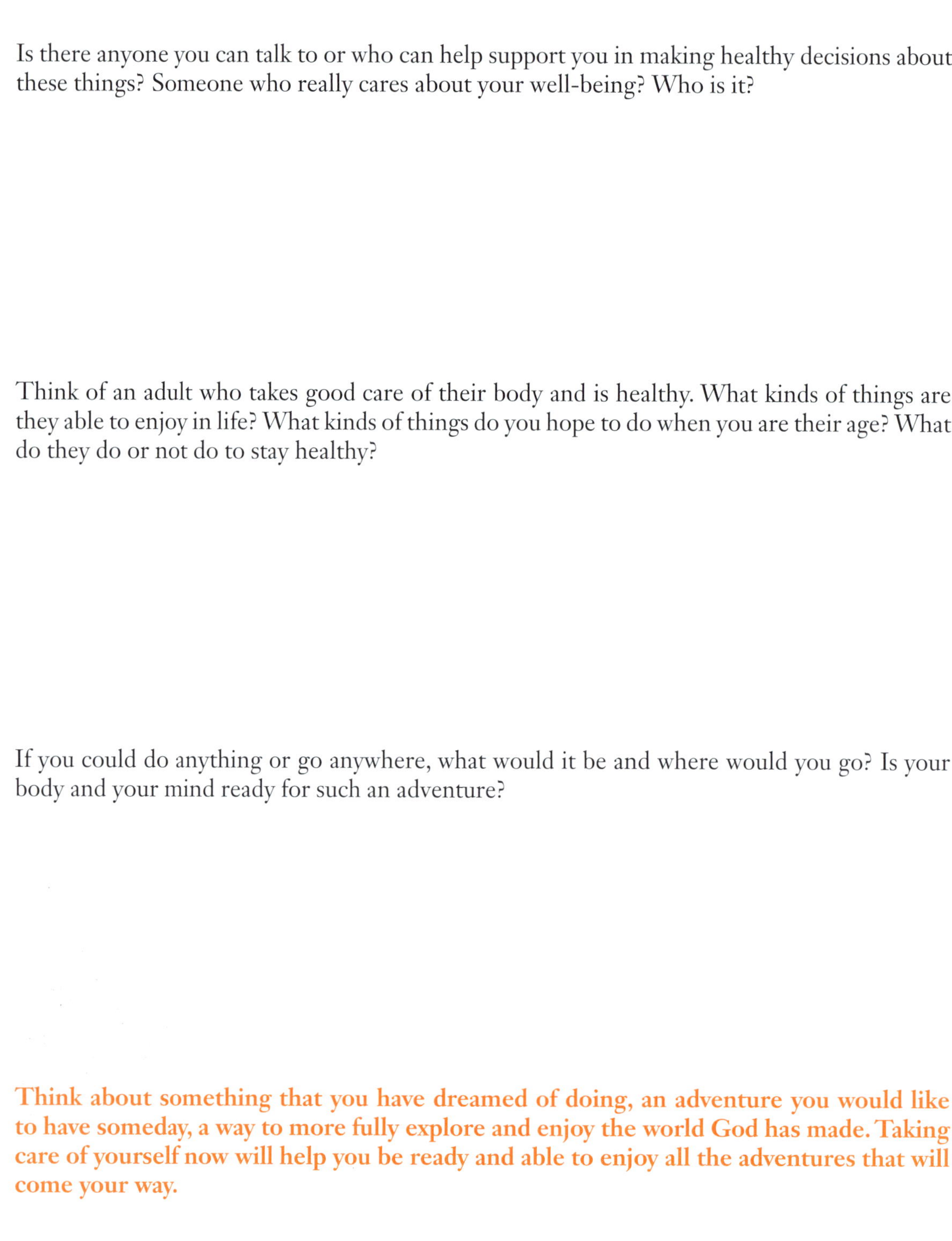

Is there anyone you can talk to or who can help support you in making healthy decisions about these things? Someone who really cares about your well-being? Who is it?

Think of an adult who takes good care of their body and is healthy. What kinds of things are they able to enjoy in life? What kinds of things do you hope to do when you are their age? What do they do or not do to stay healthy?

If you could do anything or go anywhere, what would it be and where would you go? Is your body and your mind ready for such an adventure?

Think about something that you have dreamed of doing, an adventure you would like to have someday, a way to more fully explore and enjoy the world God has made. Taking care of yourself now will help you be ready and able to enjoy all the adventures that will come your way.

SECTION THREE: **Making the Connection**

Or do you not know that your body is a temple of the Holy Spirit within you, which you have from God, and that you are not your own?

—1 Corinthians 6:19

Beloved, I pray that all may go well with you and that you may be in good health, just as it is well with your soul.

—3 John 2

Do you not know that you are God's temple and that God's Spirit dwells in you?

—1 Corinthians 3:16

For, while physical training is of some value, godliness is valuable in every way, holding promise for both the present life and the life to come.

—1 Timothy 4:8

What does it mean to you to think of yourself as a temple of the Holy Spirit? How does thinking of yourself this way impact they way you think about caring for yourself?

Why would God want you to be in good health? Explain.

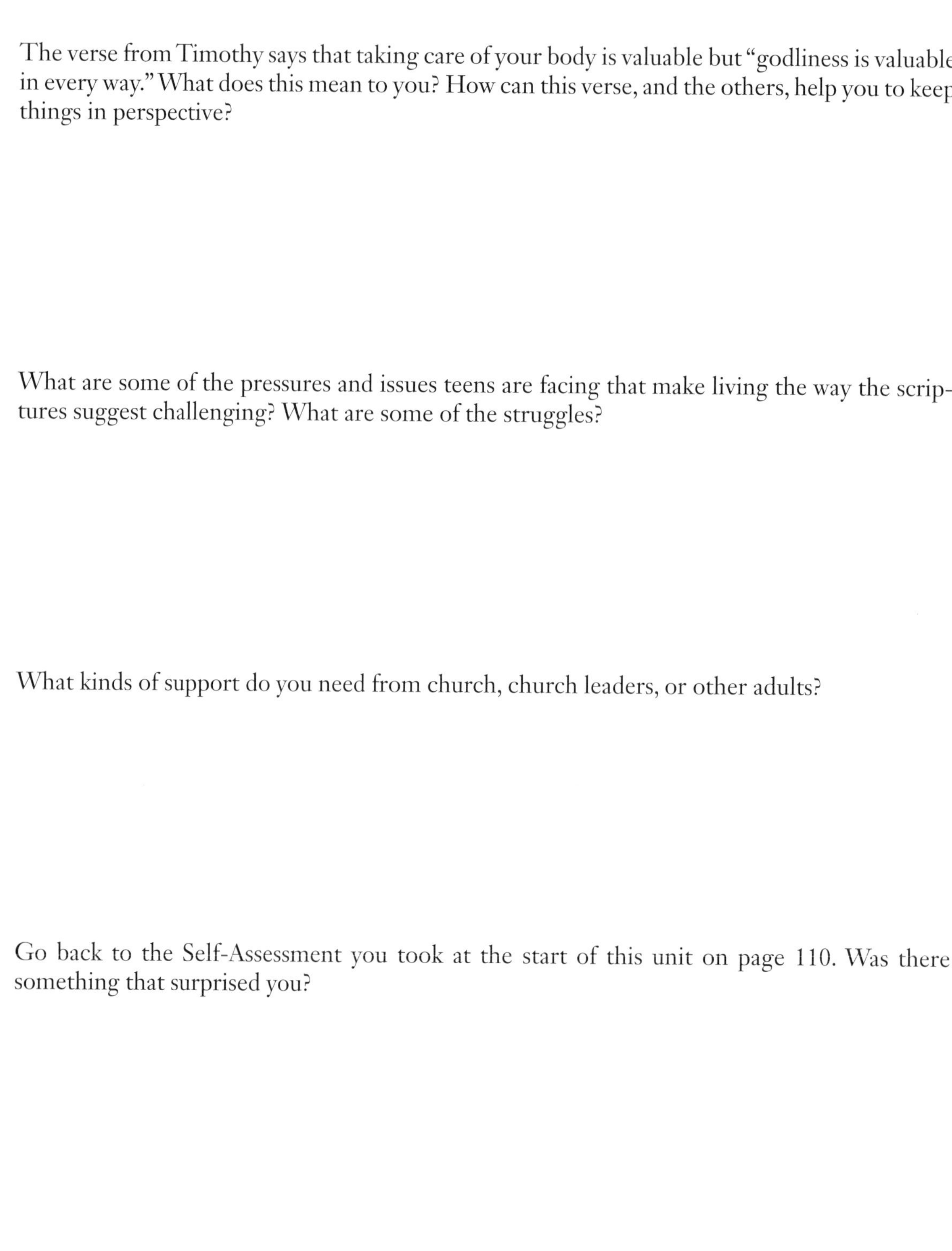

The verse from Timothy says that taking care of your body is valuable but "godliness is valuable in every way." What does this mean to you? How can this verse, and the others, help you to keep things in perspective?

What are some of the pressures and issues teens are facing that make living the way the scriptures suggest challenging? What are some of the struggles?

What kinds of support do you need from church, church leaders, or other adults?

Go back to the Self-Assessment you took at the start of this unit on page 110. Was there something that surprised you?

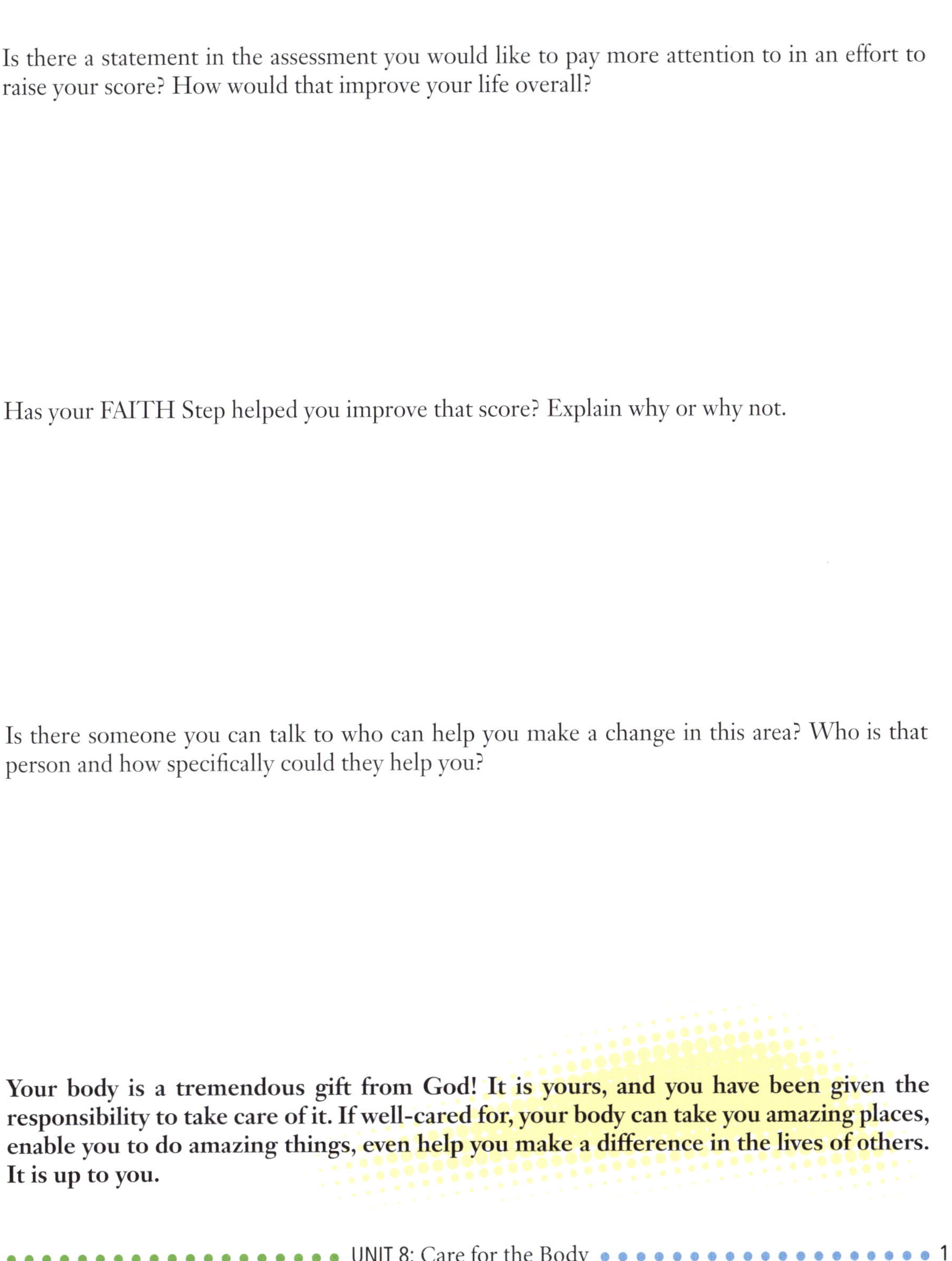

Is there a statement in the assessment you would like to pay more attention to in an effort to raise your score? How would that improve your life overall?

Has your FAITH Step helped you improve that score? Explain why or why not.

Is there someone you can talk to who can help you make a change in this area? Who is that person and how specifically could they help you?

Your body is a tremendous gift from God! It is yours, and you have been given the responsibility to take care of it. If well-cared for, your body can take you amazing places, enable you to do amazing things, even help you make a difference in the lives of others. It is up to you.

Use the space below to reflect on this section. Remember: what you write is private, and nobody should see it unless you want to share it with them.

Then and Now

You have now taken the Self-Assessments for all eight areas of well-being. You have committed to making positive changes. You have learned that being well is a journey and not a destination. We now invite you to reflect on the places you've been in the past, and want to go in the future.

It might be helpful for you now to go back and re-take each assessment. This is an opportunity for you to celebrate, to see how far you've come on the journey toward greater faith and wellness. And to see where you might want to commit to starting one new thing based on your responses going forward.

1. To begin, re-take all eight Self-Assessments. Since you are familiar with the material, this shouldn't take long.
    - Page 10: Spirituality
    - Page 22: Stress Resilience
    - Page 34: Relationships
    - Page 52: Rest & Play
    - Page 64: Handling Emotions
    - Page 80: Organization
    - Page 94: School & Work
    - Page 110: Care for the Body
2. Then, shade in the areas of wellness on the compass (on the next page) with your total scores.
3. When you have your shaded compass complete, take a few minutes to consider the questions on page 123.

Wellness Self-Assessment Tool #2

Once you have arrived at your total score from each Self-Assessment, shade in that section of the compass (0 is at the center, 50 is halfway out, and 100 is at the outer edge). Use a pencil, pen, or crayons to shade in each area with your total score (see pages 4 and 5 for examples). Your scores are not "good" or "bad," nor are they "strong" or "weak." They are simply a current snapshot of what areas of your life you have been paying the most attention to, and those areas that might be in need of a little more of your attention and commitment in order for you to be healthier.

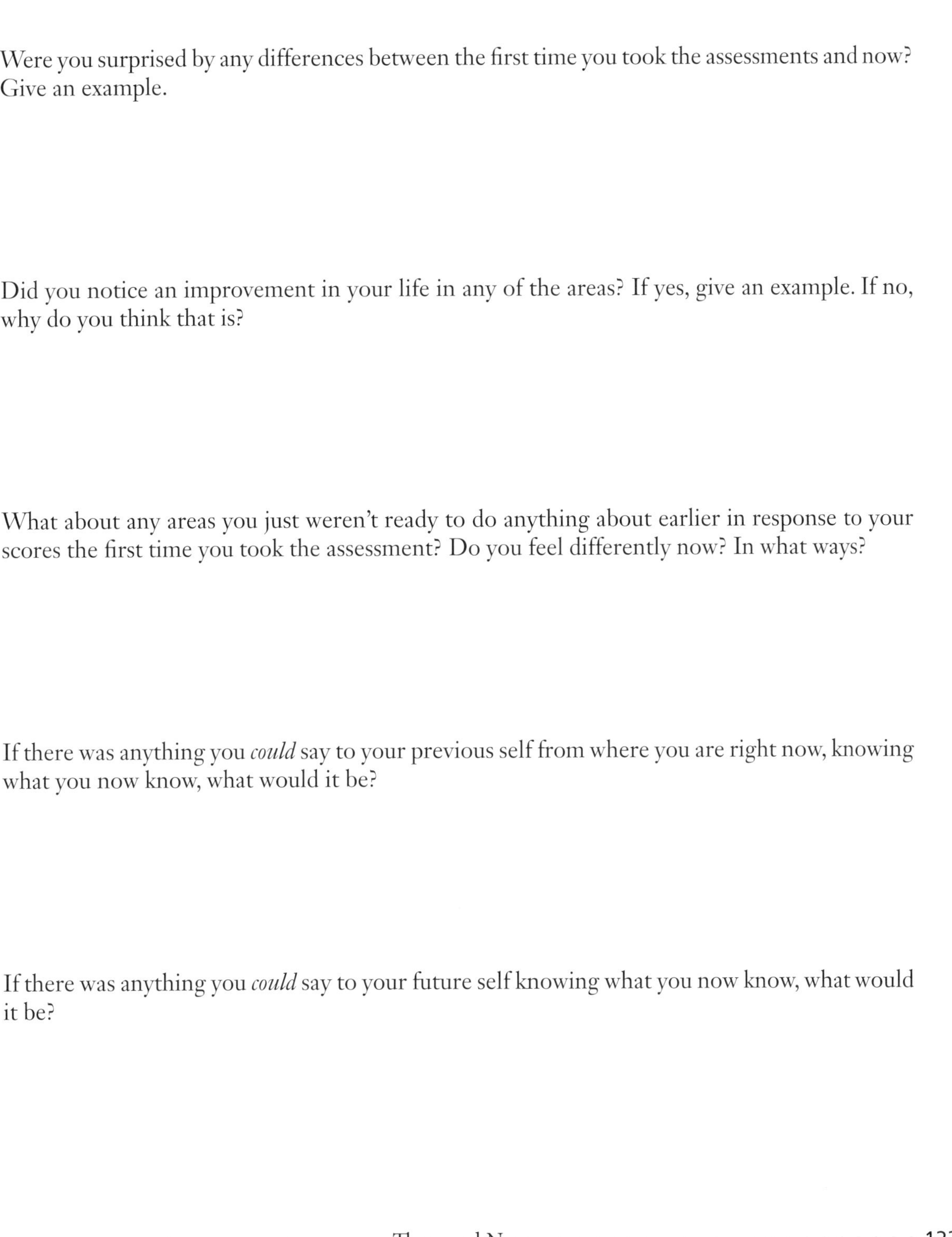

Were you surprised by any differences between the first time you took the assessments and now? Give an example.

Did you notice an improvement in your life in any of the areas? If yes, give an example. If no, why do you think that is?

What about any areas you just weren't ready to do anything about earlier in response to your scores the first time you took the assessment? Do you feel differently now? In what ways?

If there was anything you *could* say to your previous self from where you are right now, knowing what you now know, what would it be?

If there was anything you *could* say to your future self knowing what you now know, what would it be?

Where To From Here?

You have brains in your head.
You have feet in your shoes.
You can steer yourself in any direction you choose.
You're on your own.
And you know what you know.
You are the one who'll decide where to go.

—Dr. Seuss, *Oh, The Places You'll Go!*

As we come to the end of this Notebook, it's a good time to pause and reflect on this Dr. Seuss quote from his book, *Oh, The Places You'll Go!* Take some time to first reflect and celebrate the "places you've been" as you have worked your way through this Notebook. You have most likely visited some places within yourself that were new to you or were at least less explored parts of yourself.

We also invite you to reflect on the places you plan to go in the future. By now you have no doubt learned that life is a journey and not a destination. God is always calling us to grow and to become well in new ways, no matter what our age. Enjoy the journey and remember that walking with others makes the trip easier and more fun.

The quote from Dr. Seuss says, "You're on your own. And you know what you know. You are the one who'll decide where to go." The first part of the quote says that you are on your own. There is clearly some truth to this in that you, and you alone, are the one who has free choice around the decisions you make in your life. You alone decide whether you will make decisions that lead to the greater wholeness and wellness God desires for you.

However, you are not alone; God is always walking with you, always encouraging you on your journey toward greater wholeness. You are also not alone because God has created family and friends for you, and you can invite them to walk with you on this journey. Having a strong support group around you is a vital part of building a healthy, happy life.

The quote continues with, "And you know what you know." After working through the material in this Notebook, you now know more than you did about what it takes to create God's wholeness in your life. Hopefully, throughout your life, you will continue to read the Bible and other books that will increase your awareness and knowledge of how to live the life God dreams for you.

The Dr. Seuss quote concludes with, "You are the one who'll decide where to go." As you continue your journey into adulthood, this is exactly what happens. You are increasingly becoming the one who will decide where to go. As you head out on your own, remember that you will always have God to turn to as a compass—a living compass—to help you find your way.

Finally, please remember to pay attention to your life. Pay attention to the people you care about and to those who care about you. Pay attention to the blessings in your life and be grateful. Pay attention to any signs that you are not heading where you want to be heading or that your life is out of balance. Commit to living a positive life. Pay attention to whom God is calling you to be and to what God is calling you to do with your life. And remember... you can change direction at any time, and God will be there with you.

Thoughts?